Celia Louise Paris grew up on a farm in Somerset during the 1950s. She was fortunate to attend a school in her small village and, inspired by her music teacher, went on to study for a London University Bachelor of Music Degree. Teaching first at an ILEA comprehensive school and then at a convent in Dorset, she left just before the birth of daughter number one in 1985. Celia, her husband, and their three daughters have moved house fourteen times, perhaps the most unusual was to live on a boat in Essex. For the last six years, the couple have lived in France.

For Diana, Isobel and Fenella with love.

Celia Louise Paris

THANK YOU FOR MY DINNER, MAY I GET DOWN PLEASE?

Growing up on a Somerset farm in the 1950s and Early 1960s, and a family afloat 1998–2000

AUSTIN MACAULEY PUBLISHERS™

LONDON • CAMBRIDGE • NEW YORK • SHARJAH

A CIP catalogue record for this title is available from the British Library.

ISBN 9781398406032 (Paperback)
ISBN 9781398406049 (ePub e-book)

www.austinmacauley.com

First Published 2022
Austin Macauley Publishers Ltd®
1 Canada Square
Canary Wharf
London
E14 5AA

I would like to thank my husband, Graham, for his practical assistance in helping me present my book for publication, and also, more importantly, for giving me the mental space in which to compile it.

Recollections of growing up on a Somerset farm in the 1950s and early 1960s

**Church Farm
Bratton Seymour
Wincanton**

Thank You for My Dinner,
May I Get Down Please?

'When you've finished your meal, what's that piece of meat doing under your fork?'

Looking down on my plate, I see the piece of gristle which I'd tried unsuccessfully to conceal, quick as a flash I landed it deftly on my father's plate to my right. I knew he would take it without making a fuss, after all, the whole procedure had happened many times before.

Down I climbed thankfully from my chair and scampered away to play, usually in the yard or garden outside.

Farm Houses

We lived on a farm, one of three in the village, ours was at the bottom of the hill from the church and so named. By raising your eyes and standing on tiptoe, you could just see the little Norman building peeking out from between the darkness of the yew trees. My early life was really centred around the farm, the church and the village.

I mentioned that Church Farm was one of the three farms all positioned on, almost clinging to the east slope of a steep hill. The middle one was a smaller farm, proudly bearing the name of the village, Bratton, also having the oldest house dating right back to the 16th century. I remember its cool dark interior and thick walls, a slightly dapper gentleman farmer lived there in the 50s and early 60s. He had a precise way of speaking, different to the Somerset accents prevalent, and sported a waistcoat and bow tie. I never saw his wife, she must have died some years previous, but he had a son who used to enjoy playing tennis with my sister and the older girls from the school. Later Bratton Farm got gobbled up by the Manor Farm and later still, with building plots for new houses.

The first farm you came to descending through the village from the main road, was grandly called 'Manor' which I always thought sounded rather posh, but it didn't really live up to its name. The house was separated from the farm buildings by the road, which as a result was covered with mud and slush in wet weather and you had to pick your way carefully. 'Mud on Road' would have been an appropriate sign. The letterbox was fixed in the garden wall belonging to the house; in those days collections were made twice a day, on Sunday afternoons too. My grandmother used to walk from Church Farm up to the letterbox at least once a day, unless she extended her walk and went down to the Post Office in the next village. Letter writing was her only means of communication and a recreational activity in the 1950s and 60s. People wrote letters to keep in touch with their family and friends and looked forward to receiving them in return.

Anyway, back to our dining table; it was in fact an old farmhouse kitchen table with drawers, scrubbed clean every day by my mother, the wooden surface almost white. At mealtimes I sat between Gran on my left and Daddy at the head of the table, on my right. Mummy sat at the other end, and opposite Gran and me along the other side sat my older sister. Any visitor would sit next to her or spill over to our side if needed. There was a range in the kitchen, as in most farmhouse kitchens of that era, which kept it warm, so we spent most of our time sitting there in the evenings, sewing, reading, doing homework, playing cards or listening to the radio; a very large and heavy object. There was no TV until well into the 1950s, a small Bush model, black and white, of course. Most of the cooking was done on a Rayburn out in the scullery; an outhouse approached via a covered way which linked to the rest of the house. Speed was essential in transporting hot dishes, like bacon and eggs, across to the kitchen table on cold mornings, a carefully choreographed manoeuvre. Then dishes were returned for washing up in a similar manner. The scullery was an amazing place with many uses; a place for having your feet and legs washed in the big old sink at the end of a hot summer's day, a place where newly hatched chicks would arrive by post and cautiously take their first steps across the table, a place to receive boxes of beautiful white flowers at Christmas from our cousins in South Africa, and a place to welcome travellers and farm workers with some refreshment.

The kitchen had a proper larder or pantry, another common feature of the time. Ours was stacked with my mother's bottled fruits and jams, and always cakes and home produce. We had no deep freeze, so a cool room was essential, meat was stored in a meat safe; a sort of cage situated on the coldest side of the house. At supper time; a big event on a farm as it signalled the close of the working day, my father would descend the indoor staircase to the cellar and return carrying a jug of his home-brewed cider. With cheese, usually Cheddar, bread and pickles, sometimes a joint of home-cooked ham, this would be the final meal of the day, accompanied by much merriment and joviality. Visitors always recalled those times with affection and a smile. Something that used to appear at intervals on the kitchen table was the 'black box'. This was more of a chest really, shiny black and inlaid with mother of pearl. Inside were stored all the important documents and papers; a safe storage place for keepsakes. If there was a point of controversy or doubt, Daddy would ask for the black box to be brought to the table to settle the question. My sister was the one to fetch it, and many years later, she inherited it for her own memorabilia.

Church Farm was Georgian in architecture, complete (or incomplete) with bricked-up windows, a pleasing square design, evenly proportioned. From the exterior, it was attractive and well-kept, softened by a creeper growing over the front and neat little box hedges and flowerbeds and a perfectly rounded holly tree. This was the scene of my childhood play and where I learnt to amuse myself.

Inside with basically four main rooms downstairs and four bedrooms above on the first floor plus a newly installed bathroom, the farmhouse had a satisfactory and balanced feel. A beautiful oak staircase connected the levels. A further staircase took you up to the attics; these were a big playground for my sister and me, apart from providing extra sleeping accommodation. In particular, I remember dressing up in old bridesmaid dresses stored there and parading up and down elegantly. Either side of the front porch and door from the hall smelling of polish and cleanliness, the lounge was on the right; a welcoming and sunny room with a dual aspect and a piano. My father's two sisters and eldest brother played, also Mummy and her sister. At around eight years old, my sister and I started piano lessons, but that's another story. The door on the left-hand side of the hall led into the 'dining room' a rarely used room which always seemed a little damp and chilly and never in my memory served as a dining room. But I do recall it being opened up and aired at Christmas time for parties and special occasions.

Continuing down the hall and through a door into a smaller passage, the kitchen was on the right and across a passage the one-time dairy, subsequently used as a store. My grandmother had the bedroom up above, originally the cheese room. Externally, you could still see the window from which the heavy cheeses would be lowered to the ground using some sort of pulley system, but by this time blocked up with only the outline showing. Gran had her own furniture which included an attractive washstand; every morning my mother would carry a jug of hot water upstairs so that Gran could wash in her room. She was reluctant to use the bathroom even though it was just next door. Opposite to Gran's bedroom was the one that my sister and I shared. My main memory here was of a lovely surprise on Christmas Day when I awoke to see a large teddy bear sitting at the end of my bed. I still have the teddy, now a father and grandfather to all my other bears. The two front bedrooms were for my parents and guests respectively with a nice wide landing in between.

Going out of the back door and along the covered way to the scullery, there was a quadrangle of flagstone paving, framed on three sides by the kitchen wall, the covered way itself and the 'new' dairy. This area was continually in use with comings and goings and a centre for many activities as it was sheltered and mainly in the sunlight. Good for drying laundry, playing cricket or ball games, skipping, hoola hoop, gymnastics or just sitting and reading a book.

Above the scullery with its fluffy chicks and smell of cooking was the loft area. If the scullery had interesting occupants, the loft had even more. It was a useful upper level, approached via a narrow staircase and intended for storing apples and keeping things dry. However, it could, and did supply accommodation on occasions. For instance, during the war, it housed a couple of Italian prisoners for a while until my mother against regulations gave them beds in the house. Later, I remember two very large Irish 'navvies' staying there whilst they constructed a 'Dutch' barn for my father. Work was scarce and times were hard, no-one was turned away.

The cellar should have a special mention. As the house was built on a slope, the cellar was not entirely underground, but largely underneath the lounge and had two entrances. One down an internal staircase from the passage outside the kitchen and the other an external door just up from the yard. Here my father stored many things; bits of machinery, sacks of grain, tools, various nasty smelling tins and jars, and of course, his cider press and barrels.

It was here one afternoon that I received my first kiss from the younger brother of one of my sister's school friends. I remember feeling completely taken by surprise and rather shocked that he should impose himself in this way and especially as he then asked me to give him a kiss in return. I declined and sadly things were never the same again and really marked the end of a pleasant little friendship. The feeling stayed with me over the years, particularly not wanting to disturb and spoil a relationship or get too involved; all stemming from an insignificant occurrence at the age of eight.

Oh, I forgot to say, we had an outside toilet or lavatory as it was called, a little stone-built shed up the garden. It was chiefly used by Daddy and Gran; I remember them walking up the path carrying buckets of water.

Returning once more to the kitchen table, it's time to describe the diners and people who featured in my early years, so the stage has now been set…

Farm People

Born in 1881, my grandmother seemed to represent both the Victorian and Edwardian eras for me. 'Children should be seen and not heard' was one of her beliefs and sayings, although in my case, she did modify and adapt the rules a little and was surprisingly lenient and forward-thinking at times. She was born in a public house and that may have had something to do with it. At age eighteen or so she left Aberdare and 'The Bush Inn' Commercial Street (still there when we last looked) and travelled all the way over from South Wales to a dairy farm in Somerset to learn cheese making and carve a career for herself; a brave step before 1900.Her few belongings conveyed by pony and trap, she arrived at her cousin's, never to return to her home town or country to live again. Before long, she settled down and married my Grandad, and her name changed from Pitman to Day. Soon afterwards, my mother was born and then my aunt quickly followed. Eleven years went by before my three uncles arrived and the family was complete.

Dairy workers and cheese makers were still very much in the Thomas Hardy tradition in the first quarter of the 20th century, so my maternal grandparents moved around frequently from modest little cottages to grand manor houses; now extremely expensive and desirable. Perhaps, I have inherited the rather nomadic tendency.

Gran came to live with us at Church Farm when Grandad died the year before I was born. She stayed for nineteen years off and on until she passed away in 1968.The 'offs' were when she went away each year for a few weeks visiting my uncles and aunts, often by train. Before the Beeching cuts of the early 1960s, I remember the excitement of waiting at Evercreech Junction where Gran boarded the Pines Express taking her up to Manchester. The thrill of the big engine approaching, glimpsing the passengers, seeing her safely installed and shedding a few tears when waving her goodbye.

Manchester seemed a very long away from Somerset in these days. Gran didn't forget about me though, and wrote letters and sent postcards from her travels. I still have some of them. She was an important person in my early life, and we spent a lot of time together as in those days Mummy and Daddy were both busy working on the farm. She also took her fair share of household duties, for instance preparing vegetables, washing up and cleaning shoes.

Despite being very fond of Gran, I was also naughty and played her up, behaving badly on a few memorable occasions. She never went out without wearing a hat, of which she had a number for different events or days of the week – a leftover custom from Victorian times I suppose, and one I thought very silly! At the top of the village, there was a copse of trees just along the main road and one windy day, whilst on a walk with Gran, I suddenly decided to grab her hat, pull it off her head and throw it with all my might into the bushes. Oh dear! No hope of retrieving it, poor Gran, she was very cross and upset and had to walk back down through the village minus her customary hat feeling 'exposed', and with me having been well and truly told off feeling suitably ashamed.

Sometimes, as a special treat Gran used to take me into our small local shopping town on the bus. This came once a week on a Wednesday afternoon and you caught it from the main road at the top of the village. It made just the one journey there and back so you had to be 'on time'. On this particular occasion, I didn't want to leave the bright lights to catch the bus home and obstinately sat on a doorstep in the High Street refusing to move! In the end, I was probably smacked and persuaded to leave, but I put up some resistance, which I can still feel if I try hard. Of course, I wasn't taken shopping on the bus again.

But back to the table – more of a tea table now. This was my and Gran's favourite meal as there was always a good selection of homemade cakes and sweet things which we both loved. If I was good (it did happen!), Gran bought me a Battenberg cake, which was my favourite at the time with its pretty sponges wrapped in delicious marzipan, almost a Christmassy taste.

Ah, Christmas, I don't know why but I associate my father with Christmas, sitting at the head of the table, wearing a paper hat and looking a little like Old King Cole! He certainly had a merry smile, a twinkle in his eye, and what is termed as a 'dry sense of humour', teamed with a strong Somerset accent. But he did have a sterner side with quick flashes of temper and made his mind up in the first five minutes whether he liked someone or not.

Daddy had a walking stick and in mock anger used to chase my sister and me around the house if we had been particularly naughty or annoying. Of course, we could move more swiftly than him so raced up the stairs and shut ourselves in the bathroom, the only room with a lock, shrieking loudly! Everyone has a cross to bear, sometimes it takes years to identify it and sometimes it is immediately apparent. In my father's case, it was a wooden stick that was his constant companion for over forty years. I don't remember a time without it and his game leg was a real hindrance to him. Eventually, it caused him to sell the farm and move, and one stick in the end become two. Apparently, Daddy was very similar to his father in this respect, both were farmers too.

My father was one of five children (as was my mother); three boys and two girls. The Hansford family were very keen on education and Daddy's two brothers were both graduated from Cambridge. So, it was my parents who moved into Church Farm when Grandpa Hansford died, keeping it in the family for over half a century. I'm sure my father's skills with maths and money were a great asset to its successful running through some tricky times. My parental grandparents had both passed away before I was born, but the importance they placed on education and music continued into the future, benefitting both my sister and myself. We grew up with a piano in the house, my mother playing and Daddy on violin, and lots of sing-songs and hymn practices for Sunday church where Mummy played the harmonium. My parents met in the early 1930s, the first time at a dance in Bratton village hall, and then one Sunday soon afterwards when Daddy attended a service at a local village church where Mummy and her sister sang in the choir. In spite of possible social differences between the two families, they all seemed to get along well enough and some years later, Mummy's mother became a vital part of our family. I never heard Daddy and Gran exchange a cross word in the nearly twenty years that she lived with us. There might have been frustrations, but controlled, and a level of mutual respect and courtesy was generally observed.

Before my parents married, Daddy had a most unfortunate accident with a horse and cart at the top of Bratton hill. He was returning from market when the horse, always rather nervous, saw something that frightened it. My father stepped down to reassure and lead it when the horse suddenly reared and bolted down the hill pulling the cart behind it, one of the wheels going over Daddy's leg. In those days, a full X-ray was not given and only the ankle appeared to be broken, so after a few weeks, my father was back on his feet once more. The problem was actually in the hip, unrecognized at the time, but his right leg was never straight again and the ensuing limp became more pronounced giving increasing pain and complications. No more walks of any length and all slow and tedious, no more cycling and dancing of which he was very fond, and as a batsman in cricket he had to have a runner and in the end umpired instead of playing. But he still enjoyed life and got around pretty well. He liked sitting behind the steering wheel of a car where he felt as able as anyone else and didn't evoke sympathy, something that he loathed. Cricket was his lifelong passion, a member of Somerset Members Club and a keen supporter of village, county and Test Matches.

If my father was a typical Aries, then my mother was an equally typical Aquarius. She was good at making light of things, calming the atmosphere down and generally smoothing out any creases in the daily household fabric. In fact, they made a good team. But curiously, if my sister and I had a special plea or request to make, we were much more likely to have it granted from Daddy, perhaps, it was all to do with daughters getting around their fathers!

From Mummy's place at the other end of the kitchen table near the door, she could organize and serve the meals. The kitchen range was useful for keeping food hot and boiling kettles and the pantry was an essential farmhouse requirement and store. Mummy worked very hard, in the house which she kept spotless (no spiders there!), helping on the farm, mowing the lawns and tending the big kitchen garden. She made jams, bottled fruit, prepared and cooked the meals, and then there was the church and looking after people who came to stay – all done with a good humour and spirit. She was a real farmer's wife, kept hens and sold eggs for 'pin money', made and sold butter and could hand milk cows almost as fast as Daddy, about nine in an hour. She received her training at an Agriculture College near Bridgwater, where she gained certificates in both cheese and butter making, and of course, she had plenty of experience from her own upbringing before marrying. She always had time for my sister and me and we had a lot of fun together, but as she became increasingly needed and busy on the farm, I spent more time being cared for by Gran.

Mummy and Daddy had a lot in common. Even though they were not at first aware that there was any connection between the Hansford and Day families, they soon discovered that both sets of grandparents (paternal) knew each other, in fact both grandfathers had played the violin at services in Stowell church, sitting side by side in the gallery. This must have been before the organ usurped them and took the place of the little band of instrumentalists (a real Fancy Day story). Most people learnt a musical instrument a hundred year ago and could play together at an elementary level at least.

Of course, farming and a love of the outdoors was my parent's main similarity, Mummy often remarked how she would far rather be outside working than 'cooped up in the house'.

They were married for eight years before my sister Lorna arrived; a great joy to my parents and a special little friend and companion to Daddy on the farm. The two of them were inseparable and as Lorna grew older and more able, she became a valuable assistant with farm tasks, particularly with looking after young calves and the animals in general. She had her own pony for a while, until one day when it unfortunately bit her and then was promptly sold. Lorna attended the recently opened school in the village and I can remember her performing ballet and gymnastics on the lawn in front of the farmhouse. She was keen on sport and also played the piano; it was Lorna who selected the first radio request for my birthday, 'The Teddy Bear's Picnic'. Sixty years later, it is still popular with our granddaughter! Lorna's many friends from the school spent a lot of time down at the farm and helped to make it a very lively place.

As I mentioned, the kitchen table was flexible with seating, accommodating more or less in number – so who else came to join us? Well, there were the aunts and uncles; real ones, and then all the older people we used to call 'auntie' and 'uncle' to be polite and respectful. I still use these titles; an old fashion idiom hard to shake off even if I wanted to.

Mummy's three younger brothers came top of the list. When they came to visit or stay at Church Farm, it was almost like the Three Kings arriving, but separately. With their good looks and easy charm, they represented the world outside for me, bringing gifts and relating stories from faraway places –anywhere north of the Bristol Channel seemed distant and exciting. The three of them had joined up to His Majesty's Forces at the start of the War – one in each, and amazingly all three returned unharmed or mainly so. It must have been a very happy day for Gran when her family was safely reunited. She was very proud of her boys and kept mementoes of their years in the Services; I particularly recall some smart Navy-blue writing paper and envelopes with crests. The eldest of the three, Cyril, stayed in the Air Force all his life. Mummy said that he and the RAF were made for each other. The other two started new careers after the war; Ron moved north to work for Clark's Shoes where he was quickly promoted to a Sales

Manager's position. Norman, who did suffer some mental effects from the war, returned to the farming community, working up in the Midlands with milk production and cattle. I always looked forward to their visits and our kitchen was filled with the sound of fun and laughter. All three were married with families so my cousins and I met up fairly often, playing and getting along together.

Mummy's sister, Ruth had married a farmer and lived locally, their daughter was about the same age as Lorna, eight years older than me. Apart from one aunt and uncle, my father's family were more remote, an uncle in Africa, another in County Durham and a sister, unmarried, who taught in Essex. She used to come to stay in the school holidays and was good at setting me little games and quizzes to do at the kitchen table. Sadly, she suffered from a back problem which developed from a bad accident when she was a child, and meant that she was unable to stand-up straight. However, it didn't prevent her from teaching, a profession she was in all her working life. She eventually retired to a little bungalow on the outskirts of Bournemouth but held onto her piano and green Morris Minor car. Then there were the rehabs or convalescents. Mummy had an active interest in others and if she could, tried to help them in some way. So the farm become a sort of 'rest home' for friends or relations going through or recovering from a difficult time. 'Uncle' Raymond was an example – married to my father's youngest aunt (his mother's sister) and living at Chippenham. Mummy offered to have him for stays of a week or two to give my 'aunt' a break from his tedious mental condition. Nuns came, orphans, attempted suicides, and with the advent of The Hall School in the village, some girls used to come to us for their holidays because they couldn't get home, or worst of all had no home to return to. These were the war years, and the aftermath.

Of course, with Lorna joining the school in the 1940s and me following ten years later, there was a steady stream of young visitors and much fun, noise and hilarity. Saturday afternoons in particular, a large number of sports-minded girls, friends of my sister, would descend the hill to crowd around our small TV to watch the rugby, and our old hayloft above the barn in the yard would see the Guy's production in November, and the procession to escort him up the school drive ready for the 5th. The school was situated up above our farm, next to the church. A rather ugly building converted and added to as the pupils increased in number. Old Nissen Huts, timber constructions and portacabins were all used as classrooms, dotted amongst the ample grounds – kept tended and attractive with flowerbeds, a rose garden, sweeping lawns and terraces. The latter provided a splendid stage for the excellent ballet displays given at Open Days in the summer, the audience seated on a tiered metal stand watching the ballet and appreciating a wonderful view of the valley beyond. The school was loosely based on Rudolf Steiner methods of teaching with much emphasis on creativity and not so much on the sciences. Dalcroze unusually was one of the activities for younger children and later, country dancing, wood carving, clay modelling, and of course, plenty of art and music. Run by Quakers, but not overtly so, the girls attended the little church on Sunday mornings, were taught moral leadership and took part happily in the community and village life. Evacuated from Weybridge, at the start of the war, the school kept going for another forty years and ran an active Old Scholar's Association. My parents supplied milk from Church Farm to the school when it first arrived, so our links were strong. And as it expanded, and before new boarding facilities could be constructed, two or three of the seniors were housed in our attics at the farm. This was a very popular arrangement, especially as my mother always provided the girls with extra food and drinks, spoiling them a little, and when my uncles visited, a jolly time was had by all!

As a family, we were all extremely grateful to the school and for its most fortunate arrival in our tiny village – it certainly gave colour and vibrancy to the area and was sorely missed when it eventually closed.

Naturally, we had lots of local, mostly village people or farming friends who came in and out of the house daily, as well as farm workers, and the kitchen was a hub for callers. Some came on business, perhaps to take a grocery order (which was delivered a few days later), orders for animal foodstuffs, fish, meat and of course, the postman – a pleasant Scottish man called Jock who usually had a cup of tea at the table.

It sounds as if our days and lives were filled to the brim, but I spent quite a few hours on my own – 'occupying myself', originally staying close to the house and garden and within ear-shot of Gran or Mummy, but gradually, I explored further afield and became familiar with the surrounding land, enjoying the sense of freedom.

Farm Animals

The animals helped a lot – fetching the cows in for milking (over 50), counting the young steers and heifers in the field and making sure they were all there, finding my way around the yard and stalls, collecting the eggs and discovering the cat had had kittens! It was chiefly a dairy farm but Daddy also kept a few pigs and occasionally sheep – these used to try their hardest to find a way out of a field or enclosure so not a favourite. We always had a dog, a Spaniel or Terrier, and then a lovely black Labrador called Boysey. After my sister's incident with the horse, a pony wasn't suggested for me, but I did have a donkey that stayed at the farm during the winter months for three consecutive years. Sandy came from Burnham-on-Sea (where we actually lived for a short time later on). He gave children rides on the beach throughout the summer, but if you had the land and space you could apply to give a donkey a home for the winter and Daddy and a neighbouring farmer did just that. Everyone knew when Sandy arrived with his loud 'hee haw' and he ran around the field jubilantly amongst the cows. With Lorna leading us, we trotted through the fields often be-decked with swathes of Old Man's Beard and greenery; my sister's idea! But Sandy had a mind of his own and one day, he took off at a great gallop up across a steep slope, Lorna calling out for me to 'hang on'. I did manage to hold on tightly until the very last few yards before Sandy came to a halt at a closed gate. Unfortunately, I toppled off spraining my arm and worst of all, having to attend the Christmas party at The Hall School with my left arm in a sling. I was four or five years old. On another occasion, I had alighted from Sandy's back, and Lorna and I left him whilst we picked blackberries. The next time we looked, we couldn't see him anywhere and we arrived back home on foot without him. "We've lost the donkey," we announced to Mummy, who promptly gave us very firm instructions to go straight back and find him! We eventually discovered him behind a hayrick, munching happily and quite oblivious to our cries and callings! Hayricks were large round stacks of compressed hay sitting generally in the corner of fields. Summer days, evenings and sometimes into the darkness were filled with the task of haymaking. Everyone was involved and in the winter the same hay would literally be sliced from ricks, carted around the farm and fed to the cattle.

I became very possessive of Sandy and hated it when other children came and had rides. My cousin David and I used to quarrel and have 'moods' over taking turns and I particularly disliked younger girls from the school showing off (or so it seemed) on the saddle. Sometimes in the summer holidays, we went to Burnham to see Sandy at work and I had a ride on the beach but I don't know if he remembered me.

Apart from live animals on the farm, I was also the proud owner of a set of very realistic toy farm animals which I played with for hours. Up between the box hedges in the garden, I set them out in their group and herds, built my fences around them, and imagined by moving them here and there, a day on the farm. The cows were even the same breed as ours, Friesian, and the dog was a black Labrador. I wasn't a doll person even though I had a pram, preferring to put a small dog in it (we had a fluffy Terrier at the time), and push him up and down the paths. There were always cats and kittens, but really farm cats, so seldom possible to train them into proper house cats and pets. I also had a rabbit which lived in a hutch in the vegetable garden, I enjoyed picking dandelions for his food, but I remember I was not so keen on cleaning him out! My sister had guinea-pigs and I'm sure she was a better carer.

One of my firm mental and physical pictures of life on the farm in the 1950s was sitting up high on top of a wooden cart of hay drawn by a horse veering steeply down a rutted slope to pass through a gate into the lower field. It was winter time, the ground was hard with frost. No safety harness in those days, my father just said 'hang on tightly', but there was very little to hang on to! We had two cart-horses working on the farm before the advent of the tractor. They were called Tom, a large old bay and Skewbald, the colour is in the name. The blacksmith came to shoe them under the big chestnut tree at the top of our entrance, I can still smell and see the sparks from his forge. Skewbald had an heir – she became friendly with a horse from a neighbouring farm which bred race horses (Wincanton racecourse was just over the hill) and unknown to us was expecting a foal. Such a wonderful surprise when it arrived, a beautiful elegant animal, we first saw it on a misty autumn morning, so was named Misty immediately. We only kept Misty for a few months before selling him to be trained as a racehorse like his father.

Church Farm, Bratton
Seymour.
You can just see the chestnut
tree by the gate

My mother

Gran and me

My father on his Allis
Chalmers tractor

'Old King Cole'

Misty and his mother

At 'Auntie' Margaret's wedding and a bridesmaid dress that came to stay in our attic

View of the down at Bratton

The Hall School

Lorna, me and Sandy

Maureen and me

Me with Boysey and Fluffy

Farm Land

And that brings me neatly on to farm land.

Back in the 1950s and 60s, I considered any land 'mine' to walk in, pick flowers in, wade along gulleys and clamber through woods. I had no real fear of any animals in the fields apart from large bulls; it all gave me a great sense of freedom, something that I later continued on a bike. As long as I was back for meals on time, no one really worried about me and I got to know all the fields and their names and all the things to look for and where to find them; The best primroses, best blackberries, banks of violets, exotic orchids, and of course, the best routes to take. When Gran was 80, I took her on one of my special 'sightseeing' trips, over fences and up on to Bratton Down where you could get a marvellous view of the village and surrounding countryside.

I went on my earliest solo holiday away from home (I was a bit of a Mummy's girl) walking down across the fields to stay with an 'aunt' and 'uncle' on their smaller farm. Carrying a little suitcase and waving goodbye over a farm gate, it felt as if I was going to a distant land, instead of three or four fields away. In fact, you could just about see one house from the other! A couple of years later, when I was an experienced traveller, I stayed with Mummy's sister at their farm near Sherborne and also up to Shaftesbury to stay with Daddy's younger sister on their farm, so I was gradually expanding my horizons.

Of course, I wasn't always alone – friends from my class at the school used to come down to the farm for tea, and we would have fun exploring and I could introduce them to the animals and show them my favourite places. Most of the boarders lived in towns, so country life was quite remote and strange to them. I had a special friend, Maureen, about my age, the third daughter of the man who worked for Daddy on the farm. He and his wife and four daughters lived further down Bratton hill in the house which we eventually moved to when Daddy sold the farm and retired. A few years later, the whole family up and left the area, emigrating to Australia, on one of the incentive £10 tickets offered at the time.

27

From special friends to special days, the one I have in mind was a summer's afternoon in the late 50s. Glancing up across the fields we spotted a glider just about to land, silent and impressive. Lorna and I raced up the hill in time to see the pilot disembarking. To us, it was equal in excitement to a spaceship landing. We walked around in wonder and amazement; it was my first encounter with a plane of any description – and could have been instrumental in sparking off an interest in aircraft and air shows and displays, later followed up and expanded in my marriage. I seem to remember the pilot returning to the farm with us for a cup of tea, but perhaps that's imaginative wishful thinking.

Closer to home and an area I haven't touched upon, was the kitchen or vegetable garden. This was connected to the orchard growing plum and apple trees, a large plot to cultivate and maintain. We grew most of our own fruit and vegetables and only resorted to the shops for extras such as bananas and oranges; a special treat in the winter months. Mummy, of course, always made sure of her Seville oranges in January every year to make delicious marmalade. In the kitchen garden, we used to gather as a family for an hour or so on warmer and lighter evenings. Each of us had our own little plot or section to tend – Gran, Lorna and I, and a bit of competitive spirit entered too! Mummy and Daddy naturally did all the hard work – our three little gardens were just for fun, probably inspired by the school which organized a similar idea for the boarders but in their case, they were judged with a prize at the end of term. My chief memory is of mauve Michaelmas daisies which grew prolifically and filled my 'space' and of a lovely Beauty of Bath apple tree with sweet tasting fruit, eaters not keepers, that looked down on our plots from above.

Flowers from the garden and land helped adorn the church at Festivals and were useful when Mummy took her turn with an 'Altar month'.

The Church

St. Nicholas church at Bratton is an attractive little Norman building dating back to the 12th century. The entrance archway and inner door, complete with the zigzag pattern, are particularly representative as is the old round stone font (used for all family Baptisms, including Lorna and myself). There were originally three bells in the tower – the oldest dating from the 15th century, but one was certified as unsafe, so in the early 1960s, it was removed and towed on a cart down the hill to reside safely at Bratton Farm House, deemed to be a suitable resting place as it was the oldest house in the village. It was quite a momentous day; village people came out to watch the bell's progress and called it 'B Day'!

My parents were both very involved with the church in various ways. Daddy's parents had been enthusiastic church supporters and were both buried in the churchyard and some years later, Mummy and Daddy joined them with a commemorative stone marking their lives, when they too passed away. Mummy took over the organ (harmonium) playing when Daddy's sister went on holiday back in the 1930s and she was still playing it over forty years later. It didn't just involve playing; she had to pump the air in with energetic foot and leg movements too, so as she said, it felt as if she had walked a very long way by the end of a service. She also did her share of church cleaning as well as flower arranging, and used to wash the linen and clean the brass.

The flowers at Easter were especially beautiful as several people in the village, including Lorna and myself, went around the hedgerows gathering primroses which Mummy tied into little bunches, and with a backing of moss, fixed on to a wooden cross to be hung on the pulpit. Other primroses were divided up to fill small paste jars (fish and meat paste being popular) and placed amongst a moss carpet on windowsills. Local daffodils gave height and colour, and depending on availability, a few small pots of violets, and perhaps, big white arum lilies on the altar. Harvest Festival in the country was also a wonderful chance to decorate the church, bringing local fruits and vegetables as well as flowers, as gifts to give thanks for. Huge marrows and colourful apples and lots of potatoes, tomatoes, carrots and onions were arranged along ledges, steps and windowsills. They flooded out on to the porch seats to give a warm welcome to the villagers and friends. Large sheaves of corn stood at the entrance to the chancel and loaves of bread looked mouth-wateringly tempting. All the produce would then a few days later be auctioned at the village hall (later at a pub in the next village) proceeds, of course, going to church funds. At Harvest, the primrose cross was swapped for one of dahlias – very colourful and bright. Mummy always insisted that she wasn't 'in the slightest bit artistic' but I would suggest that she was. Her flower crosses and harmonium playing could really touch us all with their simplicity and sincerity. At Christmas, the little church was adorned with holly, hopefully with berries, ivy, and white Christmas roses. A Christmas tree was a later addition. It all looked particularly friendly and attractive in the warm glow of the candles.

Daddy also had his share of church duties and responsibilities; he was a Churchwarden for over thirty years as his father has been before him, and also Treasurer from time to time, his skill with money and experience with farm accounts being useful. He was a good tenor singer and the congregation at services relied on him to lead the psalms and responses. He could also manage to ring the three bells by himself, one with each hand and the third looped around a foot – quite a feat!

My parents worked closely with the Rectors over the years, finding some easier to get on with than others, but generally, the church atmosphere was a happy one and central to our lives. I have a very early memory of sitting beside Mummy playing the harmonium, and standing up on the seat pointing and counting all the people. Regular members of the congregation had 'their' pews; the Hansford pew was one back from directly beneath the pulpit, and as at the kitchen table, we had our places to sit. Gran went in first and sat by the wall next to a memorial plaque, actually for a member of the notable Angerstein family (co-founders of the National Gallery in London). The wall was painted in whitewash and bits used to flake off on Gran's navy-blue coat. Next to Gran, sat Lorna, then me, and Daddy on the end by the aisle, ready to step out and take the collection. Mummy of course, was tucked away on the organ seat or sitting beside it during the sermon. There was a Sunday School at one time, taken by the then Rector's sister, who also organized nice little cards for Mothering Sunday. Another special day in the church calendar and another time to gather primroses and violets for presenting to Mummy and Gran respectively. Subterfuge was sometimes needed to make it a surprise, for instance, quietly sneaking out of the house early in the morning to arrange the posies ready to give at breakfast.

Returning to our pew at church, smells linger in the mind and I can still readily recall that of those Sunday evenings over half a century ago, slightly musty, a whiff of polish and most of all Sunday best clothes, clean and somehow warm and reassuring. I wanted to sit next to Daddy and smell that once-a-week scent. Sunday mornings were different, I sat with Mummy, Daddy wasn't there, not sure about Lorna, but Gran sat on the opposite side of the aisle with two other blackly-clad and hatted elderly ladies, Mrs Angerstein and Mrs Smythies. Their suits and coats not just black, but shiny black with age and wear. Both ladies were extremely wealthy; the three of them together, a little reminiscent of the three French ladies in the film 'Chocolat'.

As I said, Rectors came and went, usually remaining for eight to ten years. I still have an inscribed Bible from one, the brother of the Sunday school teacher. Another, later in my life invited me to join his parish group on two occasions for trips to the Holy Land. There was (probably still is) a framed list of incumbents and their sponsors dating back to the beginnings of recorded events, beautifully lettered at first, but latterly poor attempts at the old script. Lettering was one of the art subjects taught at The Hall School; a nice extra and curiously I attended a couple of Field Study art courses in the early 1980s with the teacher from those days.

Back to the 1950s and the church at Bratton being a focal point in my early life. Summer fetes on the school playing fields were a lovely village occasion with everybody joining in. The sports pavilion was used for teas and there were many stalls, games and entertainments including a cricket match between the village team and the Hall School girls. When my sister left the school she presented them with a cricket bat as a reminder of all the enjoyable matches. The annual fete was a real meeting ground for the village and school. It ran on into the evenings with tea turning to cider and tombola to skittles. At Christmas there was a bazaar originally held in the village hall (tin hut) until that was demolished. This was my first experience of solo shopping, having saved a little money from my 'Happy' clown money box to spend on small and inexpensive Christmas presents, perhaps a needle case for Mummy or a spotted handkerchief for Daddy. Sadly, one year 'Happy' was an unhappy clown as I had a naughty habit of dropping the large china mixing bowls that were given to me to 'clean out'. When I had finish scraping them, I used to drop them on the floor, very careless! On the third occasion, I had to pay for a new bowl.

Sundays were different then, a day set apart from the rest of the week. Daddy only did what was really necessary on the farm, tending the animals and milking, and we always had a proper Sunday lunch and a quiet sit down in the afternoon. Gran used to read her Christian Herald and write letters and Mummy used to literally 'put her feet up' for an hour or so. Lorna and I had to keep quietly occupied. I usually read and in later years went out walking or cycling. Mummy related how when she and her sister were young they had to learn the Collect, Epistle and Gospel for each Sunday and recite them to Grandad Day. And keeping your best clothes for Sunday church and of course, grown-up ladies always sported a new hat at Easter. The anorak hadn't been thought of then so when your Sunday coat became shabby or too small, you wore it for play and around the farm, sleeves half way up your arms and skirts or dresses hanging down below the hem. Trousers for girls were gradually appearing in the 1950s.

On Sunday evenings after church, we usually went to visit someone – an aunt and uncle perhaps, or other relations or friends living outside the area. We had a sort of list to work through, with Gran often being consulted and very occasionally Lorna and I. In the summer, we sometimes went to visit some pretty gardens or a park. Stourhead was a lovely choice and also the walk through the rhododendrons to Heaven's Gate overlooking the Longleat Estate. Those evenings were my favourites, especially as we often called at a pub on the way home. Gran, Lorna and I were served our drinks in the back of the car, whilst Mummy and Daddy had a bit of time to themselves inside. My favourite drink (age seven or eight!) was a Babycham, which was produced by the Showering's family-owned business at Shepton Mallet. I also used to get a small bottle in my Christmas stocking: I can't recall what Lorna chose to drink but Gran would have a 'Mackeson's' which she much enjoyed. And of course, accompanied by a bag of crisps with a little blue twist of salt. We all sang merrily on the way home!

St. Nicholas Church
BRATTON ST MAUR
(modern contraction – Bratton Seymour)

Norman font

Outer porch
archway

Inner
doorway

Parties

That leads nicely on to parties, in case things are getting too serious. Both formal and informal. When I was growing up, we attended a lot of weddings – aunties and uncles, pretend 'aunties' and uncles', cousins, relatives and friends. And the ensuing receptions were jolly affairs often held in a village hall, sometimes a 'sit down' occasion, more often buffets, but with an understood schedule and recognized procedure. The welcome to guests, and line up of the bridal party, cutting the cake, photographs (black and white), the speeches and opening and reading of telegrams. Then the excitement of the happy couple's departure, usually accompanied by tins, cans and ribbons tied on the car and clouds of confetti and much advice. Cars, of course, were so much smaller; the five of us all managed to pile into a small Austin (Daddy driving with Mummy in front, and Gran, me in the middle, and Lorna in the back), remembering to lift up our feet if the roads were wet as the floor leaked!

In 1959, my parents celebrated their Silver Wedding and they had a big party at the farm with a proper farmhouse 'spread' and lots of fun and laughter throughout the long evening. I was sent up to bed several hours before it drew to a close – I was only eight after all. When I was ten I had my own special birthday party at the farm. As it was just before Christmas, Father Christmas (I later discovered he was the father of one of my school friends) made an appearance, and all the house was opened up for games, food and play. And everything looking so bright and sparkly with the Christmas decorations and lights.

In the summer, there would be lovely tea parties outside on the lawn. Gran and Lorna were particularly lucky to have summer birthdays, August 2nd and 3rd respectively, and we always enjoyed pleasant afternoons with family and friends. Mummy's sister, Auntie Ruth came over from Sherborne, and Lorna entertained us with ballet and gym in front of the house.

Every Christmas, a party was held up at the school. The first time I went, I must have been four or five years old, and had been attending Dalcroze classes once a week to get me used to school life. One of my early friends was a little boy called Oliver, and I can remember walking back down the hill after the party with Mummy when she commented, "Didn't Oliver look nice?" (He was wearing black shiny shoes with buckles) I responded, "I thought he looked a proper cissy!" Oliver and I did remains friends though until he left the school at age seven or eight to attend a more suitable boys school.

A little anecdote about dress – when I was four, Mummy had to go into hospital for a week or two and I was left in the care of Gran, an 'aunt' and Daddy. I hated it and not understanding, resented Mummy going away. Bath night was Saturday and as a bit of a protest, I stepped into the bath wearing a red velvet dress. The water turned scarlet and I got a severe telling off from both Gran and Auntie. I seem to remember that Daddy stayed quiet.

There were other people's parties as well; everyone worked and played hard in those days: Daddy's cousins at Knowle Rock Farm over on the far hill used to have a wonderful time, noise levels increasing with an accordion and saxophone, instruments played by a second cousin. Daddy used to enjoy a game of cards with Uncle Roy who was a great character, and many years later, I enjoyed several gin and tonics with him. He had a lovely rich Somerset accent and shared Daddy's 'twinkle in the eye'. Sometimes a Somerset accent was very difficult to follow, in particular, I remember an old school and farmer friend of my father's, Dougie Croft, who brewed his own cider, real 'scrumpy'. Both accent and cider were extremely strong!

Christmas time was the main time of the year for parties, which worked between families on a sort of exchange system. So we would all go up to Shaftesbury to my father's sister and family, and then they would all come to us on another evening. Similarly with Mummy's sister and family and their farm outside Sherborne. We didn't always sit at a table; it depended on numbers and how much space party games required. But at Church Farm, my memories are centred around the table for meals, with games and conversation in the lounge before and after.

Finally, just to return to that rather sad piece of meat on my plate, leftover from the beginning of this little reflection, to say there was a happier flip-side perhaps.

Apparently, I used to sit in my high chair and bash loudly with my spoon on the little tray, calling out "more beat, more beat" as I couldn't say meat! 'Seen and not heard' – not me!

The 1960s
Teenage years in the
Somerset countryside

Northacre
Bratton Seymour,
Wincanton.

On the move

We didn't need a removal van to move our furniture and possessions down the hill. Just several journeys with my father driving his tractor, things piled up high behind on a cart. Quite a spectacle for the village on an autumn day in the early 1960s, people turning out to cheer, wave and wish us well. Moving house didn't happen very often in those days – in the 33 years before I was married we moved house just the once, from Church Farm to Northacre, a move marking my father's retirement from farming.

My parents moved twice after marrying, their three homes punctuating Bratton hill at different intervals. They first lived in a new little house built into the hillside especially for them by Daddy's parents, positioned along the road from the farm, conveniently placed for my father to reach his work via the connecting orchard. It was later re-named Orchard Cottage, but as a first home for a newly married couple the house originally had the brighter and happier name of 'Sunnyside'. When Grandpa Hansford died and Grandma Hansford moved away from the village, Mummy and Daddy left the cottage and took up residence at the farmhouse, quite a big step and a little daunting for my mother.

Twenty years or so later, they moved a second time to the last house in the village further down the hill. Northacre was so named as it was built in the corner of a field called North Field. Some people tried to refer back to the old fields in the names they chose for their houses – a link with the past. In this case, 'North Field' appears on an early map of Bratton or Broctune, as it was then called. The first written record of the village actually appeared in King William I's Domesday Book of 1086, although there had been a settlement on the hillside for many centuries. Broctune literally meant 'Badgers Town', a 'tun' being Saxon for a fenced enclosure – in which these 7th-century dwellers built their huts. Thirteen centuries later, badgers still lived up on the hill behind the school, and by co-incidence, we had a family living in the village by the name of 'Brock'.

A few years earlier, Daddy had Northacre built to house a farm worker: it was a red brick construction in an L-shape. My parents decided to expand it for their retirement and fill in the L to make more of a square but then also pushed out the ends of the dining room and lounge, so finally it became a rectangle. This meant a lot of work and took several months for the builders to complete over our first winter there.

Actually, that winter was memorable for a lot of reasons, not least for the excitement of watching a virtually 'new' house being created and taking shape right in front of our eyes. The kitchen and downstairs toilet and 'wash house' were the only areas at all usable to begin with but they were invaluable. A Rayburn stove heated up the kitchen nicely and as well as a place in which to cook and store food, also housed the piano and on Saturday evenings a tin bath which we all occupied in turn. I say 'all', but that first winter we were without Gran. She went to Sherborne to stay with Mummy's sister, Auntie Ruth, until her 'room' was ready at Northacre, and Lorna had started at college in Shropshire. But Mummy, Daddy and I enjoyed those few months, remarkably mild ones that year, living in a caravan parked next to our 'new' home. Although, I had been on a couple of caravan holidays, this was quite different and special. We borrowed the caravan from a matron at The Hall School, towing it down the hill for our use until the Spring. I had my own little bedroom at one end, then there was a kitchen (not used much as we could use the one in Northacre), and a large seating area with coal fire and a dining table, even a small TV! The double bed was raised against a partition to be lowered at night for Mummy and Daddy. Mummy thought of that time as a 'holiday'; there was very little housework, no gardening (the garden was full of bricks and rubble) and apart from gradually clearing space and cleaning in the house as rooms were completed, she had plenty of leisure.

For the October half-term, the three of us, plus Boysey the black Labrador, went down to Cornwall to stay with an 'aunt' who ran a 'B&B' at Boscastle. This was another special event, as Daddy was now retired, we could enjoy a few days away. On this occasion, we very nearly lost Boysey, who decided to explore and only re-appeared just in time for the journey home. Christmas was also fun that year, with Lorna back from college to join us, and a jolly group of builders singing carols and eating hot mince pies outside.

By the Spring, we were more or less moved into our new home and getting straight, choosing curtains, wall paper, flooring and even some new furniture. The piano found its way into the lounge, and we could all wash and bath in the rather smart dark turquoise bathroom with black glass fittings. Gran returned to her 'own' bedroom, albeit smaller, but nice and warm backing onto the airing cupboard with hot pipes running through beneath the floorboards. Pleasant outlook too; from her bureau by the window she could look across and see King Alfred's Tower, a local landmark. Lorna and I shared a larger bedroom with two windows, front and side, but as she was away in term time, I mostly had it to myself. It was above the hall and had a lovely big walk-in wardrobe with two rails, so plenty of room for everything and for hiding surprises. Similar in size was our parent's room above the lounge, also with two windows; one overlooking the front and one at the other side, and at the back of the house the spare bedroom above the dining room, light and sunny with its dual aspect. Mummy was very proud of her block oak floors downstairs; she never made a fuss about shoes, but did request 'no stilettos please' on her wooden blocks, highly polished of course. Both lounge and dining room (used also as a sitting room as it had a lovely 'picture' window with a magnificent view over the valley) had grates with open fires and with the Rayburn in the kitchen that was all the heating we had for years. Sometime later, a couple of night storage heaters were fitted in the hall and lounge, but there was no central heating, and bedrooms in particular could be extremely chilly in the winter. I remember flakes of fine snow, making little drifts inside the bathroom Crittall window, and a freezing wind blowing through the ventilator above the hand basin.

Northacre was a lot smaller than the farmhouse, so we all had to adjust to living and coping in a smaller area. There were 'cubby holes' to store things out of sight, such as a good-sized understairs cupboard, a roomy pantry, an area inside the back door, and a single attic approached via a separate ladder and used only for keeping suitcases and boxes – but really nothing to compare with our previous abundance of space and very little chance to have a good game of 'hide and seek'. We still had relations and friends to stay however, and I enjoyed the company of my cousins, all growing up now so we could be more adventurous and creative, for instance, I used to play the piano for one of my cousin's ballet performances; we even charged an admission fee!

And we still had wonderful dogs – Boysey was followed by another Spotty, this time a smooth-coated Jack Russell who had an unhappy and early end on the lane outside our house and had to be 'put down'. Although he had a will of his own and could disappear down fox and rabbit holes frequently and annoyingly when you took him for walks, I was especially sad about Spotty as he was my very own dog, a present from Daddy's cousins over at Knowle Rock Farm. Daddy was not keen on us having a sequel because of our distress over Spotty, and it took him some while to relent, two or three years, but then Mummy acquired a lovely Welsh corgi (just like the Queen!) from a contact of my piano teacher at school. We all fell in love with Gwenny; she was such a good-natured dog and quickly became part of our family at Northacre for about fourteen years. But all this happened much later and I'm jumping ahead with my story.

Daddy had a proper garage 'complex' built at Northacre, comprising a spacious area for the car, a workshop, two small cow stalls, plus a separate barn for hay, and Mummy had a couple of hen houses constructed. So they could continue to 'farm' in a miniature way and feel part of the farming community, attending markets, selling eggs and butter etc. Four fields were also retained from the sale of Church Farm; eventually, we kept the two near the house, enough for six or seven young steers or heifers to run and graze in, and a few young calves too in a smaller compound. We started off with two cows, and then just one called Alice, referring to her territory as 'Wonderland! Hand-milking was always worth watching and Daddy used to be proud of his aim in shooting the milk straight from the cow to open mouths, much to the amusement of any visitors! Daddy also held onto his favourite Allis-Chalmers tractor which had many uses, including driving the circular saw belt for sawing wood, something I helped with if I was around and perhaps, started my liking and fascination for wood. The whole house was a lot lighter than we had been used to, no dark hall and stairs on which to sit during scary thunderstorms (a thing I had been used to doing with Gran at Church Farm), and of course, we missed the character and atmosphere of the old farmhouse. Mummy referred to Northacre as her 'dolls house' for many years afterwards.

The Deep Freeze

It was lucky that we chose that winter to move house, the following one was a bit of a stinker, second only to the notorious one of 1947 which my father often referred to. It all started on the evening of Boxing Day in 1962. My aunt (real one) from Essex was staying and 'babysitting' me whilst Mummy, Daddy and Lorna were out at a Christmas celebration with friends at Gillingham. When they turned to leave sometime around midnight, they found the car covered in snow, already high and drifting, and an icy slope to slither down to the road. They eventually arrived back at Bratton, managed to get the car into the garage by shovelling away piles of snow and there it stayed for about three months.

Snow continued to fall for days and with the freezing temperatures and East wind, drifted up against hedges and fences, doors and gates, and completely blocking our narrow lane through the village, making it look a little like a giant ice-cream cone overflowing. Both entrances, higher and lower, to the village were covered and impassable, so there was no access for some days for any vehicle, and then a lone tractor perhaps could push a way through. Snow ploughs were very few and far between and only just managed to cope with the main roads, cutting single tracks and carving narrow channels through the drifts. You couldn't see over the tops on either side. Of course, power lines were damaged so electricity was 'iffy', if present at all. Fortunately, we had our Rayburn and open fires, oil lamps and candles, and were reasonably well-stocked, but some outlying cottages were not so prepared, and Mummy and I, with baskets of food supplies, attempted to reach them, struggling and slithering along, trying to find the lower levels of snow. I can remember calling out to inhabitants who managed to get to a suitable fence to pass over our provisions, sometimes this 'meeting' was impossible so we had to throw things with all our might. Our Wellington boots soon filled with snow, waders would have been more appropriate. But the icy snow did give you a wonderful sense of power; walking along the tops of hedges and a 'birds eye' view of the landscape never to be matched. The silence was especially powerful and memorable and the stillness of the scene below. However, getting around was arduous and everything took a very long time, especially noticeable with the days at their darkest and shortest.

Winter feeding for the animals took on a new urgency that year, any cattle still out in the fields (the extreme freezing conditions had taken us all by surprise), were at risk of their lives, and distributing hay and fodder was a full-time job and of the greatest importance. Milking herds were kept in, and farm workers were busy around the clock tending them, cleaning out stalls and organizing dwindling supplies. Hand milking once more became a useful back-up whilst tractors chugged away generating electricity to power the milking machines. There were sad losses and no end seemed in sight.

Gran had gone to stay with one of her 'boys' for that particular Christmas but we still had Daddy's sister staying who had to return to her teaching at Romford after the New Year. The only logical way from Northacre out of the village was on foot, down the hill and taking the low road into Wincanton. My aunt was physically handicapped with her back, and although able to walk reasonably well, was unable to carry things for any distance. The trains still just ran from Wincanton at the beginning of 1963, so that was the only option for returning to London, picking up the mainline at Templecombe. One early January afternoon, it was decided that my sister, myself and my aunt, set out to cover the three and a half miles on foot, apportioning the luggage between us. All went well and our aunt caught her train successfully. Then we turned to walk home. Lorna had some experience with hitching lifts as a college student and proposed that we should return to Bratton via the top road which was a longer route; the village being in a kind of loop, approachable from two directions. But she had no intention of us walking, as soon as we were out on the 'main road' we positioned ourselves at the edge and her thumb went out and up optimistically. A few minutes later, and surprisingly, a car actually passed us and skidded to a halt, and we both climbed in. A narrow channel had been scooped through the high banks of snow, all very slippery and glistening with hard-packed ice in the late afternoon January sun. The car slithered its way along, rather too quickly I thought, bumping against the snowdrifts on either side as the young driver tried to steer a course as well as show off a little to Lorna. Fortunately, we seemed to be lone travellers on the high road for those tense eight or ten minutes, and I was very relieved when we were finally dropped in two safe pieces at the upper entrance to the village. Lorna told me not to mention the 'lift' when we eventually arrived home, I don't think many questions were asked, the main concern being for our aunt's departure. But it was my first taste of hitch-hiking, something I resumed very thoroughly some years later to great economic and cultural effect.

Talking of schools and the New Year, The Hall School in Bratton would normally have been preparing for re-opening at the beginning of the Spring term. But there was no possibility of that happening as neither staff nor pupils would be able to reach it. In fact, it didn't re-open until after the half term in the end, and I was looking forward to the unexpected extra holiday as a happy consequence of the snow. Sadly, my joy was short-lived as the Headmistress asked Mummy if Celia would like to attend a few classes in the mornings, just to keep me in a learning routine and my brain active and probably out of mischief too! Needless to say, I was not too pleased with this suggestion but was persuaded (instructed) to attend, and actually, I quite enjoyed it and all the individual attention and rather resented the other pupils returning in February and joining in on 'my' lessons. By this time, the gardeners at the school had dug a little passage through the high banks of snow to allow pedestrian access, so I used to walk up and down holding my school bag (small suitcase) of books. I didn't have to wear the uniform for those six weeks, so there was a bonus!

And then there was Lorna returning to college eventually and a little late for the new term; a large tractor came to pick her up and take her to the station at Castle Cary from where she could start her journey up to Shrewsbury. She thoroughly enjoyed the whole episode and went off to great cheering and clapping.

We were gradually learning how to cope with a very restricted lifestyle, the semi-isolation and self-reliance, and adapted quite well over the weeks until things slowly settled back into normality. By the end of February, school was back, Gran was back, and all the usual callers were back to their routines. The snow did hang around for some time afterwards and even at Easter; you could still see the remnants of the last few months when time seemed frozen in Narnia type conditions. Despite the chilblains and frozen fingers and toes, resources had been pulled and pooled together during a winter which went down in history, and was frequently referred to for many years to come.

Me and my very own Spotty

Mummy, Lorna and my aunt with
Gwenny, winter 1962-63

'Bookworm' me

Gran, aged 86 at
Lorna's wedding

Cousin Pamela and me at the entrance to Northacre. . 1963

Lorna's car with me and New Forest ponies c. 1965

June 1st 1968
Lorna & Phill's wedding
with Daddy and the cake

Mummy and Daddy outside
Northacre on the wedding day

Finding My Feet and Legs

Lorna soon acquired a little car; she was very practical and quick to pick up new skills and learnt to drive in no time. She passed her test painlessly at the first attempt, unlike me some years later. The car's arrival opened up a window in my life; in the school and college holidays Lorna and I could now go off on our own, maybe to the shops or cinema, even to the seaside, visiting people and sometimes staying with friends or relations. Of course, the car was really to enable an easier transition from Somerset to Shropshire – if its advent gave me an opening to things further afield, a much more immediate and bigger door was just about to be opened.

My sister had a dark green Elswick bicycle, a present from Mummy and Daddy, when she was about twelve. Her little car made the bike redundant, so back it came from college to reside in the garage at Northacre. One afternoon, when I was also about twelve years old, Lorna decided to teach me how to ride. I had had a bit of previous experience when staying with my Auntie Ruth (Mummy's sister) near Sherborne. My cousin's boyfriend used to run around the field behind, with me wobbling in front on an old bike at their farm. It wasn't too successful, but his instruction and encouragement probably helped to pave the way. I think Mummy was rather apprehensive of the whole idea, remembering how fearless and speedy I had been a few years earlier on a tricycle! Anyway, Lorna and I set off down Bratton hill with the Elswick; she was riding with me walking or running behind and observing her enviously. If I could master cycling, the bike was mine. When we reached the last downhill section, Lorna told me to stand astride the bike and just rest my right foot on the pedal, raise myself onto the saddle, swiftly lifting my left foot onto its pedal and with an encouraging 'you're off', let the bike do the rest. I can still recall reaching the bridge over the little stream at the bottom of the hill and calling out, "What do I do now?" to which she responded, "Start pedalling." Without thinking I did just that, my legs taking over and pedalling quickly up to the signpost, getting off, repeating the whole process several times and yelling out, "I can cycle, I can ride a bike!" It felt like magic, a very happy occasion, a big boost to my confidence and a real step ahead. For her part, Lorna was an excellent teacher and did inspire the feeling, 'you can do it'.

The bike and I became inseparable and the greatest of friends. Mummy soon got used to my new found skill and even stopped saying 'be careful' after a while. Similar in a way to my walks around the farm, as long as I was back for meals and didn't neglect my homework or piano practise, there were no real boundaries or restraints. I started exploring further and further afield, sometimes stopping off to call on people we knew and having some refreshment en route and in time, I arranged my bike rides with these visits in mind. Although, I still went on walks, cycling was so much better and quicker, and with the basket on the front, I could be useful going down to the little shop in the next village, or the Post Office, or right into Wincanton to the library, perhaps, and occasionally meet up with a friend for a ride together. I must have been thirteen or fourteen when I was allowed to cycle into Wincanton cinema on my own for the Saturday matinee. I felt very grown-up and made some of the girls at the school quite envious! Sometimes, it would be nearly dark by the time I arrived home in the autumn or winter, and a bit spooky pushing my bike up the final ascent home, with the trees overhead, leaves rustling and all rather ominous. The bike had no lights (or gears either). I remember one matinee in particular, 'A Hard Day's Night', the first Beatles film, in black and white, of course. Great fun, I saw it twice! But the teenage pop scene gets a mention later.

One of my favourite bike rides was down to Moorhayes Farm on the lower Wincanton road. At one time the train passed between the road and the farm, now famous for its special Somerset farmhouse Cheddar cheese. I used to enjoy watching the process of making the cheese and the different stages of production, also sampling bits of curd, and of course, the cheese itself. My bike basket was filled with cheese, butter, eggs and cream for the return ride home, so I had to cycle very carefully on those trips!

The basket (original wicker) was a real boon and meant my rides could be purposeful as well as pleasurable. Many years later, even when I had a car, I still went out on my bike; the initial sense of freedom and the thrill never completely wore off, it still hasn't really.

Finding My Voice and Vocation

Meanwhile, I was getting older and rising through the year ranks at The Hall School. But was I really growing up? Tending to be a bit of a nuisance in some classes, distracting other pupils, finding that I could make them laugh, seeing the funny side and dismissing certain subjects altogether. Sad to say, one of these was French, I could never see myself approaching the shores of France, having been no further afield at that stage than a few areas of the British Isles. So at age thirteen or so, I was banned from French classes, oh dear, a most regrettable step, I'm still finding out my inadequacies in that direction. At the time, letters went to and fro between school and home, and complaints were made, but my father, luckily for me, was not a great fan of 'foreign languages' and took my sacking from the French class with little fuss. Being a mathematician himself, he was much more keen that I should concentrate on that, or at least arithmetic, along with English, History and Geography and continue with my music lessons and art.

Despite this incident, I was generally diligent and interested in learning and when I focused my attention, discovered that with some application and study I could do reasonably well. However, because of my tendency not to take life too seriously, I was continually on the move between the 'A' and 'B' halves of the class, but hardly a 'moveable feast'! I didn't really fit into either section, and the moving around did cause some problems with different syllabuses and the work involved. At last, I settled fairly comfortably into the 'B' half where I sat in the front row with two or three similar-minded girls, absorbing the facts and putting my mind to the information presented, and rather enjoying the occasional praise or moment to shine.

Sometime in my early years at the school, I must have promoted a more promising aspect and given the teachers hope. As a result, I missed out a year and continued in a class with girls a year older. So when it came to sitting 'O' levels, I was allowed a 'go' with just five subjects, to see how I fared. With the two English's and History, I added Music and Cookery; the first because I enjoyed piano and had my 'theory', and the second because it was deemed to be something every girl should know, and of course, my sister was making it her career. My efforts were not so successful and must have been a disappointment, especially to the school. Cookery was another subject which I had difficulty in taking seriously, for instance putting a raw onion into my onion sauce and not being too co-operative about sharing a cooker with three other girls. This led to a few problems but my 'Afternoon Tea Scones' turned out alright in the end, and remaining behind with another girl at the end of the exam to wash and tidy up the room helped my mark. I scraped a 'Pass' with a 'Grade 6' in those days, but apart from the scones which became a bit of a 'party piece' at home, I steered clear of the kitchen for some time to come! My presence wasn't really missed as the kitchen already had three willing occupants; Mummy, Gran, and Lorna when she was around.

Oh, I should give a brief mention of Sport and P.E. lessons. Here again, I didn't follow in my sister's energetic footsteps, and it was another area where we were quite different and the school's expectations not met. Lacrosse, I disliked immensely, and can still hear the teacher running around calling out 'cradle, cradle'. Netball was slightly better and I always hoped to be picked for 'Wing Defence' where I could jump up and down pulling awful faces and distract my opponent! In the Sixth Form, which I joined for my last two years at school, I was allowed to choose either tennis or swimming as a sports activity. Neither was attractive, but eventually, I selected tennis, and made my way quickly each lesson to climb up the steps to the umpire's chair from where I did a bit of scoring and a bit of dreaming.

Yes, I was accepted into the Sixth Form with my five passes, to which I added a few more in the next couple of years and also studied for my 'A' levels. Back in the 1960s, your final two years at school were seen as a preparation and an invitation into things beyond school. We learnt a smattering of economics, typing skills, some needlework and even the opportunity to pick up a language again; I did attend some French classes, but mainly because they were taken by the Headmistress's son who was passably good looking! He also occasionally used to give me a lift back up to the school after lunch in his car, much to the annoyance of other girls: I always ran back home for lunch, originally from the farm and then from Northacre. School dinners were not appetising; I can even smell them now! The two subjects that I had chosen to study for 'A' level were

Music and History, and they are still my favourites. I had always intended to select History, but Music was a random choice and I only considered it to accompany another girl, Elizabeth, who would have been the sole 'taker' otherwise. But, as it turned out, it was the right decision for me and I had a wonderful two years, a real awakening of mind and senses, plus advancement in my piano playing. A new (young) music teacher had arrived at The Hall School and she opened my ears and my interest to a broad range of music, making it come alive, no copious notes or etching of facts, they were suddenly absorbed into our brains and there forever. It was through her that I re-routed my career path, found my strengths and weaknesses and eventually took on the tuition of others. Also, on a personal note, I was a bridesmaid at her wedding during my final year at school, my first time in that role and it marked my first visit to Colchester where I was going to spend several years at college.

My first teaching experience was with the piano, a couple of younger school pupils on a Friday afternoon, and I also managed to organize guitar groups to take part in an end of year music competition, (even though my own playing was self-taught and very basic!) My first guitar came from a friend of one of Lorna's college friends; I was very proud of it and felt really part of the 1960s. Lots of girls at school had guitars, occasionally harmonicas too on shoulder rests, playing and singing along to Bob Dylan and Donovan. Mine was given to me as an aid or diversion to relax a little and to help ease tensions caused by the build-up of school work and exams. Many years later with another guitar and in a different school, I returned to it, again encouraging small groups of players.

'60s Pop

I haven't said much about Gran lately, she was amazing really, in her 80s she was able to observe and listen without completely dismissing and although, disapproving of much of the 1960s ideas and morals, made the occasional surprising comment.

My father was essentially a Beethoven man, with a sprinkling of Chopin, and strongly opposed to the 60s musical trends. Pop groups were not in his line at all, the Beverley Sisters were really his limit, so my obsession with watching 'Top of the Pops' every Thursday evening was his worst nightmare. During that dreaded half-hour, he usually occupied himself elsewhere, but if he happened to be around, criticized and moaned. When The Beatles appeared (a frequent occurrence), he would start complaining, and on one occasion, Gran kindly responded with, "Well, they're not so bad, Dudley," that seemed to do the trick and we didn't hear so many adverse comments for a while. I suppose he reflected that if someone who was born about fifteen years before Brahms and Tchaikovsky died could still accept four young men from Liverpool with their brand of music then he should try a little harder to make an effort himself. Mummy had more of an easy acceptance of change and developments, not quite in the 'with it' set, but willing to come along with Lorna and me to see 'Help' at the cinema in Street one evening.

There was an abundance of pop groups, solo singers, TV theme tunes, and lighter music of all genres, everything from The Animals to Z Cars, much of it possible to imitate or copy on piano, especially on guitar, or at least join in singing the clear and memorable lyrics; a unique period which coincided with my early teenage years. By the time I was in the Sixth Form, my obsessive interest was on the wane and 'classical' and more far-reaching musical tastes were gradually taking over. But I had acquired a large amount of 60s pop knowledge and can still sing along to some of the songs and remember the names of the performers. If you listen to something just before sleep, it's supposed to stick in the mind, and on Sunday evenings between 11pm and midnight, Radio Luxembourg used to do a run through of the 'top twenty', starting with no.20 and working up to no.1. Lorna had a small, rather tinny transistor radio which she put under her bed covers not to be heard by Mummy and Daddy, and we listened together in the dark secretly, the volume low. On Monday mornings at school, I was very popular with girls wanting to find out the latest pop news, "Who was at No.1?" Some of my friends from class used to 'escape' down to Northacre to watch 'Top of the Pops' at 7.30 on Thursdays, and run back up the hill to be back in school for bedtime. On Saturday afternoons, two girls in particular came down for Mummy to wash their (long) hair as hair washing was only allowed once a week for boarders at that time.

I was never too keen on the Christmas party scene, bad enough when it was just girls but in the Sixth Form, boys from a couple of local public schools were invited across to The Hall School for an evening of dancing and Christmas fare. Standing around the perimeters of the seasonally decorated attractive old Music Room (usually a concert and performance room), the wallflower simile became painfully evident. The question of dress, always a bit of a worry; essentially I was country-bred, if not a 'bumpkin' as such, and at that age, still mainly dress 'unconscious'. But in the 1960s (as in any era I suppose), you didn't want to stand out too differently and there definitely was a '60s look'; rather tall and willowy, long straight blond hair, if possible with an overgrown fringe, and of course the mini-dress. I possessed neither the face, form, nor frocks and certainly not the hairstyle, so felt more than a little remote at large parties with my contemporaries.

However, on this particular occasion, I got into a conversation with a studious looking boy (nowadays probably termed as a 'nerd') on the subject of geography and maps. This was a subject with which I was quite at home and recklessly said, "Oh, there are some really good maps pinned up in our classroom," and without a moment's thought we were walking up across the school grounds to the Sixth Form classroom, a sort of pre-fabricated outbuilding about halfway up on the right. We had a look at the various maps on the wall then went through to the adjoining common room area to sit down and continue our chat. All the lights were on, of course. After ten minutes or so, we wandered back down to re-join the party, and a bit later on, I made my way home. I could report that I had survived the event and it wasn't so awful in the end.

The following morning at school, I was met with many protestations from fellow Sixth formers about the previous night and how I had 'hogged the common room' for a mere chat when others had it in mind for a little more! In my naivety, I never even considered that notion and thought the whole incident hilarious. Although I was living through the 60s and looked back on the decade nostalgically, I never really absorbed all the issues present and just enjoyed the carefree fun element, but I was growing up in the depths of the Somerset countryside so a good half a dozen years behind other teenagers.

The End of an Era

I wonder how you know you've reached the end of an era. Is there a big milestone to record the event or is it a satisfactory way to divide up your life into more manageable sections? My 'Northacre era' drew to a close when I was seventeen and about to leave home and start a new direction at college, studying music. But of course, it wasn't the end of my time at Northacre, I returned for holidays and later to live there again; 1968 was just a stretching of the ties.

There were several things regarding that year which indicated a change, some happy, some sad. As I say, leaving school, especially the same one that I'd attended for the entire twelve years of my education, was momentous in itself. I wouldn't suggest that my school years were the happiest in my life, I think those probably came a little later at college but it was still a wrench leaving. And then I was moving away from the village, my home, the church and all things familiar. My life up to that point had a certain routine and that was all going to change dramatically. Perhaps, the scenario which illustrated this the clearest was the washing up routine, with Gran at the sink, Lorna wiping up and me putting away the dishes; a picture soon to be archived.

The evenings were something special at Northacre and one of the main areas of my life that I missed the most. We all had our established patterns of behaviour: Mummy, Daddy, Gran and I, independent of each other but touching and blending at times, and these strands were most evident in the evenings. Starting with Gran, who had followed a strict code of behaviour or schedule throughout her life. Her hands were always occupied, she never just sat doing nothing, and even if the television was on, Gran would be busy on a piece of 'fancy work'. This was embroidery using silk threads, intricate and detailed with the different stitches employed, following a transfer pattern on a cushion cover, runner or little mats for dressing tables. It gave her satisfaction and a nice sense of achievement when completed and on display, either with us at Northacre or with another family member. I still have some treasured examples of her work.

At nine o'clock sharp, Gran would rise from her chair (we all had our specific places to sit) and go out to the kitchen to make a cup of tea before bed. Actually, she had several cups of tea at different intervals throughout the day, usually accompanied by her favourite Rich Tea biscuits. Mummy found this particular routine annoying and unnecessary, but as I grew older, Gran would often invite me to join her and we enjoyed a cup of tea and a chat together, best if Mummy wasn't around. Sometimes, Gran would only ask for 'half a cup' at a mealtime, so one of my amusing uncles (her youngest son in fact), gave her a half cup and saucer just for fun! After Gran had wished us a 'goodnight' and made her way upstairs, the atmosphere would change a little. Up to that time, we would all have been engrossed in our various tasks or pursuits, but sometime between 9.30 and 10pm, as if at a signal, these would be put away for the evening. I would return from practising the piano in the lounge and the three of us would become more interactive, relaxed and generally noisier. Of course, this is a picture of the darker months, not representative of summer when both Mummy and Daddy were out working in the garden, at least during the early evening hours. Mummy attended dress-making classes off and on in the autumn and winter at a local village hall. A friend would come and pick her up in a little white Mini and take Mummy and her 'antique' Singer sewing machine, along the country lanes for the evening class. These were very popular in the 1960s, and if not specifically used as places of instruction, could also be venues for 'parties', really social gatherings, displays or miniature shows. Tupperware, cake demonstrations, bread making, flower arranging, fashion and even underwear came under the 'party' heading, and housewives (normally farmers' wives) would meet up for a jolly couple of hours, and sometimes return home with some examples. No men were admitted, of course!

So, Mummy would be puzzling out some latest stage in making a skirt or dress, quite taxing for her as she was not a 'natural' – the results were not always successful but she was not daunted. Alternatively, she knitted, and during one winter produced a whole pew-full of cross-stitch kneelers for the church. She also tried a bit of rug-making with Readicut wools and a metal hook device for pulling the thick thread through the canvas. I can remember a particularly attractive swirly patterned rug in a half-moon shape lying in front of the lounge fire. It was certainly the era for hobbies and there weren't many idle fingers around. And in between all these activities, there was the fire to keep going, supper to get, (Daddy liked holding out his brass Armada toasting fork towards the glowing coals for toast) and any chores such as ironing, to complete. Mummy didn't have a lot of time for reading although she could recall books readily enough which she had enjoyed. I think she was afraid of immersing herself too much in case she was neglecting something else. Later on in life she did turn more to reading when she had less 'duties' and could 'settle' as she called that happy state.

By contrast, when he retired from the farm, Daddy loved reading and made up for lost time. He joined the little public library in Wincanton and on Friday afternoons withdrew his book selection for the week. Quite limited in those days, the library was basically one small room of the Town Hall, positioned underneath the Town Clock which was rather grand and noticeable as the building stood on the lower corner of the High Street where all the A303 traffic had to travel pre by-pass days. It was a miracle that it never got hit by the big lorries, swinging around the bend. A few years later, the library moved further up the town to smart new spacious premises opened by Princess Margaret. I also joined the town library with Daddy and we used to vie with each other on the number of books and authors we had read; Thomas Hardy, Agatha Christie and the adventures of Sherlock Holmes were a few of our favourites. Daddy particularly enjoyed crime novels, but also more serious reading such as J.B. Priestley, A.J. Cronin, and even a bit of Dickens. Television programmes were selected so didn't interfere with work or hobbies or take over our lives, and sometimes we had the big old wireless set on instead.

But to begin with at Northacre, Daddy took on a part-time job sorting out a farmer's accounts, and brought great bundles of papers and ledgers home to work on in the evenings and gradually get into order. And then there were the church accounts too, an on-going occupation over the years.

So, around the big dining table during the early evening, the three of us would sit, individually absorbed, and Gran beside the fire with her needlework. Mummy sat at one end with her sewing machine, Daddy at the other end with his papers and me along the side between them with my homework. We had a long school day and quite often I didn't arrive home until nearly 7pm, then a quick 'high tea' and out with my books. After homework, came piano practise, although in the Sixth Form, I was able to fit some time in during the day in a special little wooden piano hut with a desk, away from everyone else, deep in the school grounds. In fact, it became known as 'Celia Hansford's room'!

Back to the evenings and practising piano in the lounge at home, often a chilly experience with the night storage heaters at their lowest ebb. Sometime before 10pm, with Gran upstairs getting ready for the night, I would return to the dining table for a special time before bed. Daddy was a keen card player, and apart from whist (probably his favourite game but requiring four players), he enjoyed a game of cribbage. He taught me to play and for 10 or 15 minutes most evenings, we had great fun together with shrieks of laughter and 'hoorays'. Mummy liked to hear us play, and it did provide a good winding down and relaxation at the end of a day. I usually followed it with a hot drink, trying different 'brews'; Ovaltine, Horlicks, various chocolate drinks, to prepare me for sleep, but when in bed of course, out came a book which I probably wouldn't 'put down' for another half-hour or so. I was called a bit of a 'bookworm' but have continued to find great pleasure in reading all my life.

Another little side issue regarding bed times and rituals; Gran possessed very little money, only her pension really, but would insist upon popping a half-crown piece under my pillow. These were lovely 'silver' coins worth two shillings and sixpence in the 'old' money (about twelve and a half pence today). On the occasions she did this, I used to knock on her bedroom door and try to smuggle the coin back when she was otherwise distracted. This 'performance' went on many times, often several during one 'goodnight', until Mummy intervened and told us both to get back into our beds. Gran had many interesting items in her small bedroom, including beautiful old writing books filled with Grandad's elegant script, all smelling of lavender and Eau de Cologne.

And it was these evenings and scenarios that I missed upon leaving home in September 1968. Things were never the same again, but some things had changed prior to that September, and it all happened so quickly.

Lorna had got engaged to be married the previous year and then suddenly, she settled on a wedding date, June 1st and all was bustle and preparations. Northacre was 'open house' for many weeks before and after the wedding at Bratton – and I had to retreat back up to the school for any quiet time to revise for my 'A' levels. Everything was bedecked in white ribbons for 'The Day', including Gwenny the dog. I was the chief bridesmaid, a role I didn't really relish, but all passed off reasonably smoothly on what turned out to be the hottest day of the year, with the service up at the little church on the hill.

So then we were four, with Lorna's departure and removal of her belongings, the house seemed empty, bare and rather silent. In particular, I regretted the loss of her lovely Bush record player and her collection of World Record Club records. Gran and a few other ageing friends and relatives attended Lorna's wedding at Bratton, looking back over the photographs recently as the 50th celebrations took place, I was reminded of the people and history surrounding them. Daddy had some elderly relatives present, or at least, representatives of their surviving families, and of course, Gran was there as the oldest surviving relative on my mother's side, aged 86. The very oldest person that I knew had died by that time, an aunt of Daddy's who married a farmer at Stowell, had nine children and then retired to Milborne Port where she lived with one of her daughters and son-in-law, both around 80 years old. Aunty Doll as she was known, closely resembled Queen Victoria, was born shortly after the end of the Crimean War (so the same period as Florence Nightingale), and lived to over 100. Gran always enjoyed visiting Aunty Doll as she 'made her feel quite young'.

A couple of months after Lorna's wedding, Gran was taken poorly and had to go into hospital, she had a tough life in her earlier years, bringing up a family on an extremely tight budget, putting up with harsh conditions and generally working hard. She lived for another two or three weeks but very sadly passed away at the end of August. She had just celebrated her 87th birthday. It was such a shock for all her family but especially for Mummy who had shared her home with Gran for the past nineteen years. As her bedroom was cleared and her bits and pieces divided between the five children (Gran had been meticulous about labelling everything so there would be no fuss), it really did seem like the end of an era, and of my life up to that date. I wandered around the house listlessly, no Loma with all her jollity, and now, no Gran with her companionship, reliability and sincerity. But there was still a certain whiff of Eau de Cologne in her room and especially, in the wardrobe, a sort of lingering spirit to remind me of her. After a while, I moved into Gran's old cosy bedroom for the winter months, and the scent was still vaguely noticeable.

Gran's funeral was a big affair, the service was held at Stowell and she was buried alongside Grandad in the churchyard, just opposite the church porch. They had lived at Stowell when they were first married; this was the little church with the gallery where Mummy and Daddy's grandparents had played violin back in the 19th century. We used to take Gran over to Stowell several times a year, to the church and to tend the grave and we continued with these visits in later years, taking flowers to place on their combined grave. Gran was keen to pick bunches of the big white daisies in the summer to put on Grandad's grave as these flowers were his particular favourites. The little country church was packed for Gran's funeral service, and led by a vicar with a marvellous voice, looking a bit like Ken Dodd with his rather unkempt hair. He also played the organ and infused the rousing Welsh hymns with great energy, lifting our voices in memory and praise to Gran and all she stood for. I remember, it was a warm late summer afternoon and the door was open, letting in the sunlight and the people standing outside to join in the service.

They say that things happen in three's; that was certainly true of that summer of 1968. We had only just completed sorting out Gran's room and possessions, when it was time for me to start packing up to leave Northacre for my first term at college. Sixteen weeks sounded a very long time and Essex seemed a very long way away. I was afraid of forgetting how Mummy and Daddy looked or even their voices and had serious doubts about recognizing them again, no internet connections in those days. So, that was really how my Northacre years closed, but not entirely ended, rather like a reference book, it was there in the background, a firm and reassuring anchor and point to come back to from wherever my studies or work took me. It was always my home, and the people were always my people, the village, the church, and the surrounding countryside were deeply etched upon my mind, my character and my life.

A Family Afloat ~ 1998–2000

MFV Thorntree
The Boat Yard
Maldon
Essex

Cast Away

It all began one wet weekend at Weston-super-Mare in the Spring of 1998. Graham bought a couple of boating magazines for amusement and we all started to dream…

I knew nothing about boats, just an occasional turn around the bay or up a river with my father or a friend rowing on a summer's afternoon, but the concept held a fascination and gave rise to romantic ideas. Graham, fortunately, came from a nautical background and had much practical knowledge and experience to offer, especially, having already lived on a boat and handled barges on the French canals. We held Diana's singing of John Ireland's setting of Masefield's 'Sea Fever' as a sort of shining beacon to guide us ahead and the girls started collecting Arthur Ransome books.

We were running out of money and time at our flat in Weston and a move was in the wind when the 'Boats for Sale' advertisements came before our eyes. Each one was filled with mystery and excitement and suddenly all five of us were involved. A tight and low budget had to be adhered to, and although not serious just 'looking', some parameters were soon put in place … 'Is the galley so important?' 'How many berths do we need?' 'Do we really need an engine?' 'What are the Heads?' And more importantly – 'When can you use them?' A new vocabulary was introduced, one smacking of adventure, distant horizons and life on the high seas. Graham was there to modify our thinking, to restrain and advise and talk sense on necessary features and size. There was such a range of styles, shapes, materials and uses, whether you were stationary or on the move – and how you moved – power or sail and if so, how was the boat rigged? Lots more questions followed – 'what does full rig mean, or gaff-rigged or Bermudan?' And a spinnaker looks fun—

We got carried away into another world, and lots more boating magazines were to follow over the next few months. The advert pages became a series of rings, arrows and pen markings as different ideas and inputs were considered and added, and tastes and requirements were slowly refined.

And then there was the question of location; we were initially looking at the whole of The British Isles, poring over maps and working out logistics. Choices and decisions were dependent on the coastline, geography and weather conditions of particular areas, and we soon learnt the basic differences between the East and West coasts for example. Muddy river estuaries, rocks and tidal ranges all had to be seriously considered and the sort of boat best equipped for each.

Timing was another issue; how long would it take a family of five to pack up and leave, not just to 'downsize' but to virtually finish one life and start another? Perhaps, we should simply sit it out and wait patiently for our fortunes to change. Friends and relations thought the whole idea slightly crazy – we had done a few unorthodox things before but maybe this notion was a bridge too far and in reality, was it the best plan or right decision to make?

By this time, both Diana and Isobel were attending music school at Bushey, with Fenella to follow in September, and it was already April. Much to be organized and many things to settle in the next few weeks, it seemed a lone voyage even before we had started out.

'Silver' at Brentford Canal
A John Bain Design

Red Herrings

As new ideas and specifications were lining up and becoming more definite and serious, it was time to acquaint ourselves more closely with a few boats.

Needless to say, some of these were totally impractical and disappointing to view, others could have suited our needs and pockets, but were unfortunately far too small to house our effects, even with my intention and plan to dispose of the bulk of them.

One of the first visits we made was to the Thames near Windsor to see a very nice river cruiser, well equipped for two but impossible for five – despite its alluring attraction of built-in bookcases to accommodate two hundred odd books. We held an interest on the Isle of Skye for a couple of mad weeks; a Motor Fishing Vessel (MFV) ready for conversion and in an attractive spot… here the enticement was the use of a Bechstein piano and living in a caravan ashore whilst working on the vessel. Idyllic summer weather naturally assured…! Next, we were back down to the inland waters of the Brentford canal and the elegant lines of a classic Silver yacht; beautiful to see and feel, the three girls even had their photo taken sitting in the saloon.

The location didn't seem to feature too much in the early days of our search although ultimately it was probably the most significant factor. The next flight of fancy was down to Devon and Cornwall, areas that Graham was particularly familiar with from some years previous aboard his parent's boat, West Breeze. A couple of lovely days out, just three of us now as Diana and Isobel were back at school. Graham, Fenella and I clambered high up to the decks of wooden ships lying stranded on the bank of deserted creeks, stepped gingerly onto boats afloat and in one sad case almost submerged from recent flooding, and expressed many 'ooh's' and 'aah's'. One of our most adventurous and memorable visits was down to Southampton to look over a huge wooden Danish MFV. Space would have been no problem here, we approached the vessel by dinghy, then a mixture of climbing up a ladder and being hauled on deck, and what a deck, vast and similar to a ski slope and slippery even in summer; all this for a bargain price, but another dismissal from our listings.

Barges were another fascination and absorbed us, me especially for a while, and still do at times. I dreamed of Bruges, my barge be-decked with flowers, bikes, perhaps a dog and grand piano and even contacted the Field Study Council to suggest a possible liaison with hosting one of their specialist art courses. And closer to home with more modest proportions, we all pictured our ideal narrow boat personally customized and decorated, but then realized this could result in five boats, a family convoy sweeping up and down the inland waterways.

Thinking was finally directed towards larger and more commodious boats that could still move around fairly easily, and converted MFV's or a motor sailor seemed more realistic and appropriate. From the logistics point of view, we decided the east coast would be a useful mooring and with this in mind, one day we set off for the estuaries of Essex, a county both Graham and I were familiar with, in fact, Graham was born at Dovercourt along the coast just a few years earlier!

It turned out to be a day that was to change our lives quite dramatically, interrupt and break the established and accepted pattern of selling one house in order to purchase another, and incidentally at the same time rewarding us with a thick album of souvenir photographs. Leaving Weston-super-Mare early one morning in May, Graham, Fenella and I motored across to the opposite shores of England to looked over an MFV moored at Maylandsea, a small village on the southern banks of the river Blackwater. Fifty-three foot in length with a fifteen-foot beam, smelling of highly polished wood, Thorntree appeared attractive in the Essex sunshine. Constructed just after the Second World War up in Scotland of thick wooden planking, a curved canoe stern and decorative sails, I was impressed by her looks and romance, failing to see the flaws. I started to picture us all living aboard, working out the sleeping arrangement, birthdays, tea parties on the deck and sailing merrily down the river – here again as in previous reveries the weather was perfect. Graham was more dubious and frankly not so keen and we returned home in the afternoon to continue our search through the adverts.

As the days and weeks slipped by, time became pressured with the sale of our flat proceeding and Fenella due to join her sisters at Bushey for the start of a new academic year and the requirement to be settled and within easier reach of the school. Graham was continuing to work at a retirement home in Weston and I was continuing to home educate Fenella until the end of term, but in between, the idea of Thorntree kept re-occurring. She was the only boat as far as I could see that we could all move onto and was in any way in a fit state to accommodate us, remembering that Diana and Isobel had not even seen her and had to rely on our description and opinions. I was getting panicky to say the least. So one day, when Graham was working and Fenella was outside playing, I phoned the broker making a provisional offer – he phoned back a little later to say the owner would accept, and suddenly we had acquired a boat! There is no going back on boat offers and with his acceptance all was settled from that moment on. I rather nervously telephoned Graham at work to inform him of this new acquisition; he was quite stunned I think, but after the initial shock rallied well without any recriminations.

All was now 'full steam ahead' with preparations, starting with placing up to thirty advertisements a week in the local paper to sell furniture, crockery, toys, Graham's planes, even some music and records and clearing the flat of sundries. A host of antique and second-hand dealers descended and amazingly most items were sold swiftly and easily. Some things, mostly books that I couldn't bear to part with, we packed into boxes to store in a friend's attic until we could house them properly and others were surreptitiously transported up to Bushey where they resided in the wardrobes and cellars of the school until we retrieved them later on. The flat became a sorting office with all the comings and goings of collection vans and payments, but within a month or so most items had been disposed of. By the time Diana and Isobel returned for the summer holiday, the onetime cosy flat was quite empty with only the essentials remaining.

The piano was a tricky decision. Eventually, we placed it with a Company near Oxford, to be 'swapped', or part-exchanged for something more suitable when we were ready and settled. This could mean renting a room for practise purposes or even a wooden shed, but definitely and sadly, the Young Chang grand piano that had been with us for fourteen years, had to go, although we did manage to hold onto it until the very last minute. With three daughters, all pianists and requiring daily use of a piano, this was a problem of crucial significance, needing to be resolved as soon as possible.

It was quite an exercise in getting rid of items and also in trying to view everything objectively. As the departure date loomed nearer, there were many 'goodbyes' to be said, and a few tears were shed. We were, as a family, all very much attached to the Parish church of St John's in Weston, a focal part of our lives with the three girls in the choir and regular Sunday attendances. In fact, this closeness with a church community was hard to replace in the future, and as time went on, we never really did. Then there were the local shops, parks, the seafront, and the library in particular, which had been invaluable during the four years of home education.

But we were eventually more or less ready to go and hired a van (not big enough) to transport our much-reduced belongings across to Essex. At the last minute, the final packing and disposal of bits and pieces became almost overwhelming, and our downstairs neighbour kindly came to the rescue with a calming cup of tea and haven for the girls to sit and recover for the journey. The 'new' owners of our flat were already waiting in the garden, so we had to push on and make our exit as swiftly as we could. Graham drove the hired van with Isobel and Fenella beside him in the front; Diana and I followed in the large and rather daunting Citroen XM, surrounded by tightly packed luggage, and only just able to see out and operate the controls. There was no time to look back; the road ahead took all my concentration, remaining energy and determination.

Welcome Aboard

We made one stop on the way to our new home, at the makeshift South Mimms Services on the M25, pressing on to arrive at Maylandsea before dark. No satellite navigation in those days, just maps and memory from the only visit we had made a couple of months earlier.

It was now mid-July, the weather was hot and heavy, so it shouldn't have come as a surprise that as we approached the Marina, the evening sky darkened dramatically and a few spots of rain started to fall. Necessary and vulnerable items such as duvets, suitcases, food and household provisions were hastily unloaded, and we all ran along the pontoon to step aboard Thorntree. The thunderstorm quickly ensued as welcomes and assistance were given, and the girls were introduced to their new way of life. From the start I observed the drips, where they appeared and how to place small trays strategically below each, but, surrounded by the soft lights and glowing wood we settled down around the table; one of two in the saloon, for our first meal afloat. We still have treasured mementoes of that evening; the girls presented us with two candles, one a star and one a fish, and an accompanying note of 'Thanks' for taking the adventurous step to live on a boat.

And then it was time for bed. At Maylandsea, there were 'facilities' so we could all go along and use the showers etc, and if the tide was 'in', our Heads could be utilized. As for berths, Graham and I had decided to sleep up in the deck saloon which had a convertible sofa, quite comfortable but a bit of a palava to convert to a bed every night. The girls used the berths below deck – Diana on a single and Isobel and Fenella sharing a plush double opposite, both with portholes and separated from the main saloon by a door. The Heads – toilet, wash hand basin and a shower (actually unused by us during our time aboard), and a sort of store were situated in the fore-peak, and there was a ladder from there up to the deck. Aft, and below the deck saloon in Thorntree was what seemed like a huge engine room where the excellent Perkins resided, also the generator plus water and fuel tanks, and the whole area later benefited greatly from a clean-up bestowed by Graham. A few boxes of books were initially stored here but met with disaster during wet weather early on, and I sadly lost some much-treasured volumes this way. Rather ironically, I recently found my 'water-marked' copy of 'Captain Noah and his Floating Zoo', one of the surviving casualties.

It was warm and cosy aboard with three diesel heaters, in the girl's cabin, the saloon and deck saloon; the one in the saloon was also handy for heating up saucepans or kettles. A raised coach roof with surrounding portholes was a great asset in the saloon, giving extra light and good headroom. The galley was adequate and served us well with a small Calor gas cooker. We housed the little fridge up in the wheelhouse, neatly fitting it beneath the helmsman's seat. The wheelhouse was positioned centrally, an attractive angled shape with an entrance door on both sides, a place to hang coats, and a useful mirror. My favourite place was probably the deck saloon; you could sit up there viewing the shore, absorbing the sunshine and light, read a book, listen to music, or just sit enjoying the ambience, feeling detached but not apart.

We were only at Maylandsea a few days before it was suggested that we move upriver to Maldon and civilisation. I was a little reluctant to leave so soon, as I felt we were on a holiday amongst the yachts and pleasure craft at the smart marina. But we set off one morning on the tide, our first adventure afloat as we didn't know anything about our destination, what to expect or even what the next few hours would bring.

We were not disappointed though, approaching from the river, Maldon is particularly attractive, with the rise of the cottages up towards the little church, a few Thames barges drawn up alongside the historic quay, the working atmosphere of the boatyard, and the river dotted with small craft and shaded blue by the brilliant July sun. We were guided to our berth at the end of some rather dilapidated wooden staging (pre-pontoons), and a couple of hours after leaving Maylandsea, we were safely attached to our new moorings. The boatyard at Maldon was a much more vibrant place, a mix of craft, all sizes and conditions, and Thorntree took her place among them very comfortably, adding to the picturesque scene. Artists congregated in the town especially by the waterfront and Thorntree became a popular subject for painters.

At the end of 'our' staging, there was a photographic studio and also an artist who collected wood and debris from the shoreline, using them to create sculptures, collages and designs. Maldon is famous for its mud – a memorable texture, colour and smell, teeming with a unique world of small creatures and plant life. Graham had a closer look whilst working on Thorntree's hull; scraping, cleaning and painting. We soon started to settle in and find our way around, becoming familiar with the boats and their owners, discovering the pros and cons of living aboard and making the necessary adjustments.

A first sight of Maldon

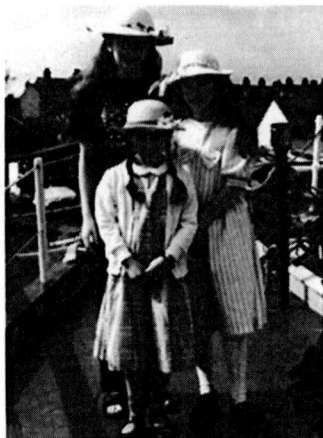

Thorntree berthed at Maldon

Thames barge on the Blackwater

Thorntree on the high seas

Sailing weekend

Watercress almost R.T.G

Bella Pais

Mrs Thorntree

Perhaps, the biggest adjustment to living on a boat, even a fifty-three foot one, was the organization and deployment of limited space. Taking the idea from the previous owners of Thorntree, we supplied the girls with a blue plastic container each, to be filled with their most valued and treasured items, excluding books which were a separate issue, also their numerous dolls. All three girls were fond 'parents' to dozens of dolls and over the years had built up quite a collection. Given names, which Graham and I were supposed to remember, they accompanied Diana, Isobel and Fenella everywhere, part of daily living and almost 'human' with their individual characters. Much to Graham's annoyance and possible embarrassment, these dolls were lined up around the deck in full view of the boating fraternity, and little plays and stories would be enacted. On one sad occasion, a member of the doll family accidentally fell overboard; cries and tears of distress followed from Isobel and Fenella, but Diana very swiftly changed into her swimsuit, jumped into the less than pristine water of the river and swam out to rescue her. She returned to great applause and joy and was certainly a hero for the day!

Thorntree had a spacious foredeck, plus a smaller deck aft, and to begin with, we housed many items under tarpaulins awaiting a placing including five bikes, a bookcase, suitcases, and other bits and pieces and equipment. I painted the deck (or most of it) one fine day – a special sort of red earth colour paint-cum-sealant preservative – it looked good if a little slippery at first. The bikes were soon taken ashore; four deposited in the 'shower that wasn't' in the boatyard toilet block facilities, and my very old 1950s Elswick in the large boat work shed where it gathered dust and cobwebs during our sojourn at the yard.

Very fortunately, a month or so after our arrival at Maldon, Graham was offered a 'proper' job with a water company near Manchester. This meant he was away for periods, occasionally up to a week, so we 'girls' had to learn to cope on our own and make sure everything was 'shipshape'. Replenishing the water tank was one chore; connecting a hose to the main's tap ashore and remembering to turn it off when the tank was full. Another, not so pleasant job, was getting diesel fuel for the heaters; the 'lucky' person had to descend a vertical ladder into the engine room from the wheelhouse, fill a jug from the fuel tank and extremely carefully, without spilling, carry the jug back up the steps. Diana was very good at this task, nice and calm with a steady hand. She also had a go at climbing the 'ratlines' of the sail masts on deck, a long way up, but with a bird's eye view of the boatyard and surrounds.

Later, we decided to dispense with the huge main mast, which was actually damaging the boat with its weight and had it lifted out at another yard along the river. The tan coloured sails did look attractive but served no useful purpose, and Thorntree was much better off without them. Her engine, already mentioned, was reliable, good and powerful.

Other skills the girls learnt during our time afloat were the ins and outs of tying knots and some of their names, varieties and uses. Along the quayside, a couple of people had set up a display 'stall', and on fine days would sit in front of the Thames barges demonstrating their knot-tying skills and selling small products such as hair slides and key fobs. I think we still have one or two of their exhibits. Of course, ropes were a progression or sideways step from this, and essential knowledge to boat owners. The girls learnt some basics from Graham: how to tie a bowline, reef knot and perhaps his favourite, a 'round turn and two half hitches', and I'm sure the beauty of coiling a 'cheese' on deck will not have been forgotten! But the speed and dexterity of using ropes to secure a boat to its mooring was more problematic, and I don't think we ever succeeded in performing this task to Graham's approval. He visualized and dreamed about a silent, swift and secure performance to the admiring glances of nearby spectators! However, early on, we did all learn to appreciate the benefit of fenders.

We also had a useful dinghy housed on deck and lowered into the water by ropes on a pulley system.

Row, row, row your boat

Much fun was had with this, the girls learning how to row and step in and out of the small bobbing craft quickly and assuredly, going off on their own for short distances, usually with a group of doll passengers. Occasionally, they rowed up the river to the local Tesco's, mooring the boat and doing some shopping. On one return trip the tide had risen and they had difficulty in coming back under the low bridge, eventually, feeling and pushing their way out with the oars on the stoned roof above. In the following August, the three girls and a friend attended a weekend course organized for young aspiring sailors on a lake at nearby Heybridge, and gained some practical experience in handling Mirror dinghies – what to do and what not to do. Fun, if a little tense to observe, but perhaps not such fun afloat going full pelt towards the shore, and the odd collision and bruise occurred.

The first summer on Thorntree was certainly an experience for all of us, filled with new ideas and activities, some most enjoyable, some slightly less so.

There was a wash block portacabin near the end of the staging that we generally used, preferring to keep the 'Heads' on board for emergencies or night-time, but if you wanted to have a shower, there was a more distant facility situated along the quay. Both 'blocks' required a key to enter, and I still seem to possess mine! So, in the evenings between seven and eight o'clock, Diana, Isobel and Fenella could be seen making their way reluctantly, towels over their arms and carrying sponge bags, up past the Chandlery, down by the pub, towards the shower block, five minutes or more away. The showers were not welcoming; often very grubby with big spiders on the walls, and quite chilly in the winter months. However, if you could ignore these things, the water was good and hot and the actual showers worked well. Washing machines were here in this building – you needed tokens to operate these, purchased from an office opposite on the quay – and also large sinks which could even accommodate sails. All the visiting boats and barges could use these on-shore facilities, hence the problems with maintenance and cleanliness.

When the girls packed and departed for school, it seemed very quiet, especially with Graham at work, and I found myself spending days alone for much of the time. But I was finding my feet and making acquaintances in the boatyard and up in the town.

The little kiosk selling tokens for the washing machines doubled up as a river police office and I whiled away many a half-hour chatting to the man in charge, supplying a flask of coffee when the power was 'off and a piece of cake or mince pie.

My first 'port of call' upon leaving the boatyard for the shops would be the Chandlery. Our mail was delivered here, and it was an essential place to find and buy any bits of boating equipment. Most boatyards and marinas had Chandlery's but the one at Maldon was particularly good and helpful to us 'newcomers'. Continuing up the hill, Dagger Lane joined the High Street which was typical of a smallish market town, with a nice mix of shops, an excellent Emporium, an ice cream parlour, a couple of 'chain stores', two book shops, two or three charity shops, the Post Office, banks and a new library. The Co-op food store was very handy, and I became a regular customer during our time in Maldon. Here, the till ladies quickly discovered that I lived aboard, and immediately named me 'Mrs Thorntree' which I didn't mind at all! I also used to walk from the boatyard along the footpath to Tesco's, through a little park, passing the houseboats with their pretty flowerpots and awnings, crossing over the bridge and then leaving the river at the last minute to scramble up the bank to the supermarket. This scenery has mostly and sadly disappeared in recent years, with the building of expensive houses, the disappearance of the houseboats and the 'cleaning up' of the area.

In the afternoons, I much enjoyed sitting up in the deck saloon, reading, often with the sun streaming in; warm weather would see me outside on my deckchair chatting occasionally to our 'neighbours'. When the girls were back on holiday, we borrowed story tapes from the public library and the four of us would sit up in the deckhouse listening drowsily during winter afternoons, anything from 'The Railway Children' to 'Watership Down'. Of course, we had my favourite Radio 3; the radio reception and stereo sound were superb on board Thorntree, the wooden interior creating a marvellous acoustic. Choral Evensong was particularly impressive, even inspiring me to take the girls on the bus to Chelmsford Cathedral one afternoon to join in with a live broadcast.

Millennium Christmas cake

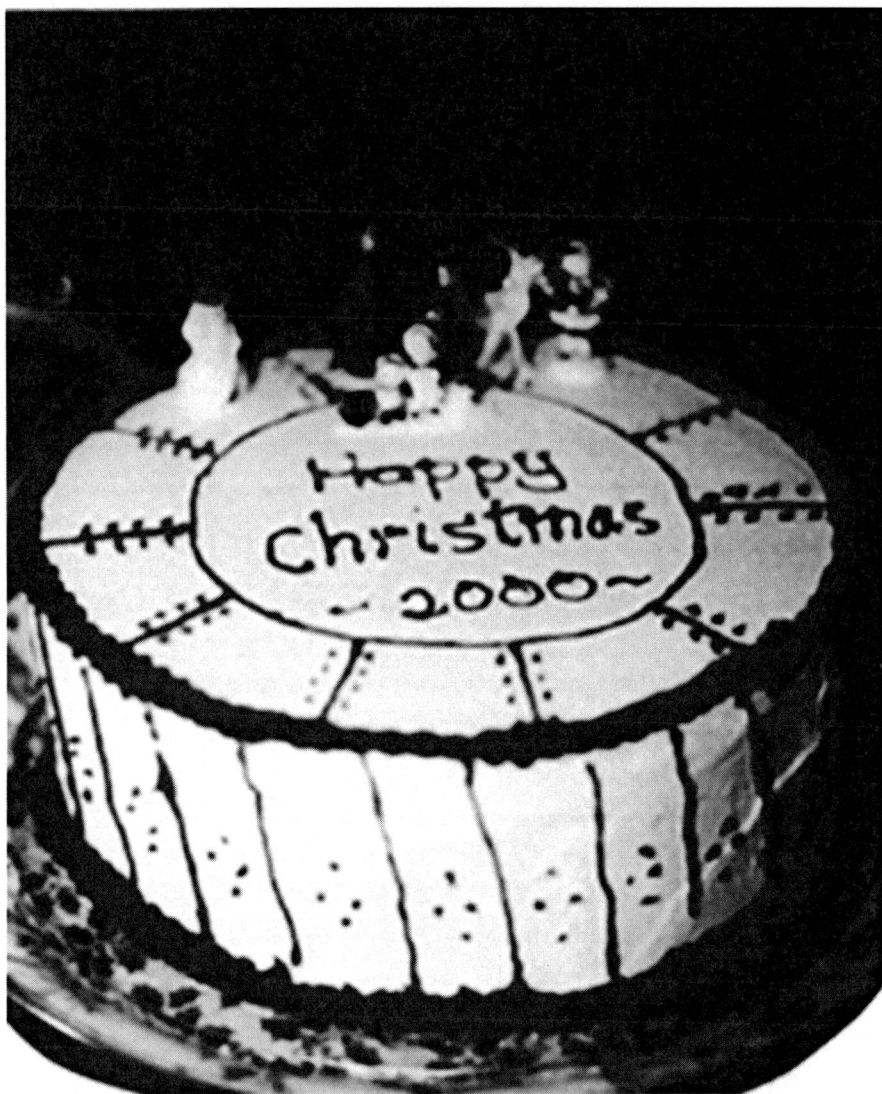

And then there was Boris, the boatyard cat, or as 'big John', the resident shipwright on the yard used to term him 'neither a cat nor a dog.' He was a companion to us all and a real character, took to sitting on Graham's father's cap in the wheelhouse, or on the top of the companionway steps giving occasional swipes as we passed up and down. He did get a sharp reprimand one evening as we were all eating a fish supper to which Boris was magnetically drawn, so he was a little warier after that for a while. The girls were especially fond of Boris and amazingly, Isobel managed to lift him up and settle him in her doll's pushchair, before carrying the whole thing up to the deck, with no complaints from the occupant! At night, if I was going to the boatyard facilities, Boris would race me back along the staging as if participating in a playful game. He did, however, sometimes like to surprise Graham and me with an early morning gift, tapping on the deck saloon window and threatening to bestow an unfortunate little bird on our bed; a nasty habitual instinct belonging to cats, but we managed to dissuade him on a couple of occasions.

Christmas 1998 was a special event on Thorntree; we bought a green ornamental fir tree with red decorations and fairy lights and set it up in the saloon. The decorating extended throughout the boat and the lights in the deck saloon above were so enhancing and attractive that we kept them in place for the next year or so. Boris found the idea of a tree onboard very tempting but he soon learnt to leave it alone.

We spent two Christmas's afloat and eighteen months living aboard Thorntree. The second Christmas we were invited as a family, to supply the music, chiefly carols and Christmas musical arrangements, for an evening's entertainment at The Little Ship Club to which Graham and I belonged. Based around the piano, Diana, Isobel and Fenella playing various instruments; violin, clarinet, recorders plus percussion effects, and even Graham joined in 'O Come all ye Faithful' on trumpet! It was an enjoyable and memorable evening, with the festive singing and good cheer, rounding off with an excellent supper and sprightly 'Pass the Parcel', including some interesting 'forfeits'; we still have the little silver clock that Graham won for his rendering of The National Anthem in the style of Elvis!

Christmas on Thorntree

Boris

Land Ahoy!

Living on the boatyard amidst the atmosphere, talking and thinking and gazing at boats, it was inevitable that various 'rescue' projects came to our notice. One such abandoned endeavour was a little sixteen-foot plywood day boat, with a planing hull and cosy interior, in fact, she was first called 'Oh so cosy' and then the present owner re-named her 'Watercress'. Graham couldn't resist taking her over, she came 'free' but did possess an outboard motor which we acquired later on. This was an extremely powerful 55hp Yamaha, heavy to lift but certainly moved Watercress along fixed to the stern, almost lifting her out of the water, even with the five of us on board. After a few weeks, she was ready for launching and took her place on an inside berth in the yard. She was painted a smart dark blue and seemed to shine as she skimmed across the water. A favourite trip on Watercress was back to Maylandsea on the afternoon tide, just making it over the causeway, brewing up a cup of tea, and then returning to Maldon on the same tide. Heybridge Basin was a nearer destination, more for a lovely summer's evening. Watercress was just the right size for the girls to sleep aboard, giving rise to talks of adventures and poetic thoughts.

We also ventured forth with Thorntree on two or three occasions, going as far as Osea Island in the Blackwater, where we anchored off and used the dinghy to row ashore. Graham and Diana celebrated an April birthday on one of these trips – I have a vivid picture in my mind of Isobel and me each carrying a birthday cake, candles alight, up the companionway steps to the 'tea party' in the deck saloon, singing of course.

Another memory of these steps was of a Sunday morning, the three girls and Graham sitting around the table below eating croissants, and myself bringing the full pot of hot chocolate down from the deck saloon and slipping on the descent, bumping from step to step. But I landed safely, holding the glass pot well aloft in front of me and sat down to finish my breakfast to some applause!

During our second year afloat, various factors indicated that we really needed a shore base. Graham's work was too demanding and involved to prop up a boating venture, however much fun, and the girls' workload and dedication to their future musical paths were being undermined by a somewhat haphazard existence. The phases of the moon and whims of the weather should not really affect our daily lives, so Thorntree was placed in the hands of a broker and we would have to wait and see the outcome. Although many sea-worthy improvements and beneficial 'live aboard' necessities had been carried out, she was still quite an undertaking and challenge.

Early in the New Year 2000, we received an offer not to be refused and went ahead to complete the sale a few weeks later. In the meantime, we had been fortunate to rent a small flat in the town, above a hardware store, owned and run by very pleasant and helpful people, and just right for our purposes. My grand piano had morphed successfully into a Yamaha U3 upright, which I still possess, a real warhorse and highly valued for its service to both the girls and my subsequent teaching. That had been installed (with difficulty) into the upstairs flat from the very beginning and was soon joined by the rest of our effects, either on crowded display or in boxes, with the added encumbrance of beds and linen. We also gradually retrieved all our 'extras', both from Weston-super-Mare and the school cellars, books and pictures adding to the melee. I was teaching piano to a few students by this time, from in and around Maldon, and I had to work a little magic every day, transforming the flat from a rather domestic bedroom scene into a serious teaching area. Graham had his 'office' computer area, which doubled up as a large wardrobe and storage room, and we all coped exceedingly well with just the two rooms plus a small kitchen and bathroom. Mrs Thorntree became a familiar sight to-ing and fro-ing between the boat and flat with various bags and containers of food and the occasional saucepan!

Aboard Thorntree, we had an electronic keyboard which served us well until we started renting the flat, and saw the formation of my early little nucleus of students, given a very helpful boost by an adult singer who lived just up from the boatyard and was looking for an accompanist. I still keep in touch with him and another of my adult piano pupils from our days in Maldon.

Lights out – summer 1999

In the summer of 1999, we experienced the total eclipse of the sun standing on the deck of Thorntree. A friend was visiting at the time and we all watched together the silent passing of the darkening shadow, in a way, a sort of fitting and thoughtful epitaph to the 20th century, seeming to have an almost spiritual significance.

For the Millennium itself, we all attended the big Diocesan Service at Chelmsford Cathedral; the building was packed, and afterwards, the Bishop led us into the town (now a city) to hear the bells ring out for the start of the new century; it was a cold starry night with clear skies.

We certainly had our ups and downs with Thorntree; an 'up' in altitude was the evening we decided to view the Maldon summer fete and fireworks from the deckhouse roof, neither too strong nor stable. After we had climbed the ladder and arranged ourselves aloft on chairs, the roof was never the same again and the deckhouse itself suffered some nasty leaks in the next storm! And I suppose, a definite 'down' was the afternoon when Graham was talking intently with a fellow mariner on the very wobbly and basic staging, and took a step backwards, falling slap down onto the mud, but unfortunately hitting his side and back on a rope, interrupting his descent and cracking a couple of ribs. An evening at Chelmsford hospital followed, but no really serious problems ensued thank goodness, apart from having to resist all laughter for the next few weeks.

January 2000 saw us packing up ready to leave Thorntree and depositing our things in boxes and containers at the flat; by now bulging with our belongings, and any extras spreading out onto the landing. We stayed on in these rather cramped conditions until the summer, when we finally moved back into a property of our own in Colchester. But we continued to enjoy the boatyard, still going for trips on Watercress, and Graham even purchased another 'rescue job', this time a day boat called 'Bella Pais' which we found abandoned in a field near Maldon. She was another wooden boat but had an interesting history; when new, she was presented to a Governor of Gibraltar upon his retirement, General Sir Dudley Ward. Luckily, we held onto and still possess the original logbook. Bella Pais was a bigger project which kept us occupied for the next couple of years, finishing the restoration work and eventually, launching her into the River Colne at Alresford Creek, further up the Essex coast. We got to know some of the Essex rivers and estuaries fairly well. One of our favourite all-day excursions aboard Watercress and leaving about 4am on the tide, took us down the Blackwater and then turning north to West Mersea; a most attractive little inlet and harbour. It was actually situated on the west coast of Mersea Island, which, as an island, could get cut off at certain times from mainland Essex.

We were all sad to leave the nautical scene and atmosphere at Maldon; the yard, all the activity, and Boris, of course, but did keep our interests and connections with the water for the next few years, and even now, I sometimes have dreams of returning one day. The girls will probably always remember the names of a few boats from our time there: I once wrote a little 'missing letters' quiz for them to have fun with at school, and they did well at filling in the blank spaces. Most impressive were the big Thames barges, a dozen or so historic and picturesque vessels; Reminder, Xylonite, Hydrogen and Pudge and all the others. Every year a barge race was held on the Blackwater, the girls 'betting' good-humouredly on the winner. And then there were all the smaller craft and yachts moored around us – Sea Pig, Amaric, Craig Dubh, Makalu and Firefly, each one instantly bringing to mind both the boat and its owner.

Our final morning on Thorntree in January 2000 dawned snowy and slippery; it was the first snow we had encountered in the almost two winters since arriving. When the new owners and dog stepped aboard, Graham stayed to guide them downriver to their overnight berth at Bradwell before they set off for Lowestoft and Thorntree's new mooring and final destination the next day. I journeyed over in the car ready to drive him back to Maldon. As I watched from the shore, suddenly all the memories of the last eighteen months or so came flooding back; the shared family experiences and a way of life I knew could and would never be repeated.

Thorntree on the beach

Guiding Watercress to her mooring at Maldon